FLOWERS   VITREOUS ENAMEL ON STEEL   20 X 34 INCHES
Collection Helen B. Warner, Irvington, N. Y.

CHARTREUSE PLAQUE   SGRAFFITO TECHNIQUE 18 INCHES IN DIAMETER
Collection Col. John S. Sullivan, Washington, D. C.

ENAMEL ART
ON METALS

Edward Winter

WATSON-GUPTILL PUBLICATIONS
NEW YORK

TO

THELMA FRAZIER WINTER
whose inspiration has left its mark on this book

Copyright 1958 *by* WATSON-GUPTILL PUBLICATIONS, INC.
New York, New York
Designed by Ernest W. Watson. All rights reserved.
Library of Congress Catalog Card Number: 58-8128

PRINTED IN THE UNITED STATES BY CIVIC PRINTING CO., INC., NEW YORK, N. Y.

FOREWORD

Ernest W. Watson

In 1941 I had the pleasure of interviewing Edward Winter and writing an article in the *American Artist* magazine about him and his creations in vitreous enamel, under the title, "Edward Winter Opens Up New Decorative Vistas."

At that time Winter had been working in this medium professionally only ten years, experimenting, discovering, and succeeding to such an extent that already, he had achieved national fame; his art was being sought by architects, decorators and manufacturers, as well as by hundreds of buyers of the smaller objects sold in quality stores throughout the nation.

Seventeen years later Winter continues to open up new vistas, finding exciting new applications for his colorful art in unaccustomed fields, thus bringing it into competition with glass, marble, terra cotta, stainless steel, aluminum, plastics and other modern materials employed in building and decorating. In so doing he has lifted enameling technique out of its one-time connotation of a small jeweler's craft, into a practical, large-scale medium suited to architectural decoration and utilitarian objects without losing the jewellike quality of this ancient craft. This has been the result of an almost fanatical zeal working nights at the huge furnace of the Ferro Corporation of Cleveland which, during the day, is occupied with the manufacturing processes of that company.

It is one thing to have the imagination, the talent and the stamina to produce such a vast amount of enameled work ranging in size and character from ash trays, bowls, plates, and plaques to large-scale panels for the interior and exterior embellishment of hotels, restaurants, stores, and public buildings; it is another to find a market for it. This, also, Edward Winter has done without the help of either promoters or salesmen. Through his own industry his work has been exhibited in over a hundred museums, universities and galleries and, unassisted, he has accomplished the distribution of his smaller work among retail buyers throughout the country.

And now, through the teaching of his fascinating craft in the present volume, Edward Winter has put the delights of vitreous enameling into the hands of even beginners; he has demonstrated how with very simple and inexpensive equipment the novice can produce small objects of great beauty and permanence.

Winter has always had the desire to share with others. In 1935 he taught the first class in enameling at The Cleveland Institute of Art and thus introduced the craft into public schools through the teachers who studied with him and learned how to bring it within the reach of high school students. Since then he has further developed and simplified the processes that are revealed in this book so that vitreous enameling is among present-day crafts open to students and hobbyists alike.

Edward Winter and his career are what we like to feel are typical of American genius and American initiative. Ed never had things easy; whatever he has done is the result of unremitting industry. He had to help himself through school by working at all manner of menial work. His ambition never took account of money or the lack of it; what he wanted to do he has done. He attended The Cleveland Institute of Art for his basic art education. After graduation he determined to go to Vienna to study pottery and sculpture, even though he had scarcely a dollar to his name. He found five friends who had faith in him and two hundred dollars that they were willing to lend. So, in 1931, he sailed for Europe.

In Vienna he became interested in the enameling art and devoted himself to learning the various techniques of an art that had been practiced in Egypt, the Orient, and in Greco-Roman times. His career was now oriented; he would bring home with him the basic knowledge of the craft that he had acquired in Vienna and develop it into broad areas of use hitherto undreamed of.

Upon his return to America a door was miraculously opened for the achievement of his ambition. Mr. R. A. Weaver, the president, now Chairman of the Board of the Ferro Corporation of Cleveland, whom he had met shortly after his return, became interested in this brilliant young artist and was sympathetic with his ambition. He offered him the use of his experimental laboratory, which provided the means for producing large enameled panels in its huge furnace.

In discussing the possibilities of vitreous enamel, Winter calls attention to its application to steel, cast iron, aluminum, and other metals in modern technology, as well as to the traditional copper, silver, and gold. He envisions the function of the modern artist as all-embracing, concerned with the over-all problems of designing, materials, production, promotion and marketing. He emphasizes the importance of direct handling of the medium, rather than working from drawing board sketches. The day of the cloistered artist, he maintains, is past. The creator must have knowledge of and control over every operation from the conception of an idea to the delivery of the product into the buyer's hand. This is the way he has made the name "Winter" synonymous with the art of enameling in America.

It is scarcely possible to speak or write of Edward Winter without reference to a very talented wife, who has achieved a reputation as a ceramic sculptor and painter which matches that of her husband as an enamelist. Ed and Thelma are indeed thought of as a team, each complimenting the other in diverse talents and each fortifying the other in the creative and practical problems of their professions. And so the last word should, in the spirit of gallantry, be addressed to this remarkable lady, Thelma Frazier Winter, whose contribution to her husband's career should not be underestimated.

ACKNOWLEDGMENTS

Those persons named below are but a few of the many who have influenced my life and my career, and have assisted in the creation of this book. To all I express my appreciation for their encouragement.

Mr. and Mrs. Worcester Reed Warner, who helped finance my education; Henry Turner Bailey, director of The Cleveland Institute of Art in the late twenties; Julius Mihalk, instructor of the school, who suggested I make enameling my career; Winifred Robblee Mitchell, treasurer of an architectural firm that helped finance my European study; Otto F. Ege, dean of The Cleveland Institute of Art, who invited me to teach its first classes in enameling in 1934-1935; Robert A. Weaver, Chairman of the Board of the Ferro Corporation, who offered me the use of his company's research facilities; William M. Milliken, director of The Cleveland Museum of Art, who instituted the first Enamel on Metal Section in that Museum's "May Shows" in 1933 and awarded the first prize to my group of ten entries; Anna W. Olmsted, director of the Syracuse Museum of Fine Arts, who first featured my work in the Second National Ceramic Exhibition in 1933 and all succeeding shows thereafter; J. E. Hansen for technical proofreading of this book, and his nominating me for the Charles Fergus Binns Medal which was awarded to me by the American Ceramic Society; Ernest W. Watson, who featured my early work in the *American Artist* magazine and who designed this book; Thomas E. Thompson who manufactured the fine transparent enamels I have used; photography by Robert C. Hoffner, Marion Greger, Betty Norton, Parade Studios, Blanch and Richard Godfrey of The Cleveland Museum of Art.

Contents

Student firing a smail enamel brooch with a propane hand torch.

INTRODUCTION:

THE URGE TOWARD THE CRAFTS

An urge toward the crafts has a long history in America, dating back to early colonial days when craftsmen brought their skills with them from their countries of origin in the Old World. What they brought, however, and what, through the years, grew from it, relied almost entirely upon traditional designs that had been handed down from father to son.

Colonial craftsmen often created from necessity. They had no great department stores in which to buy their furniture, dinner or glassware, wrought-iron weathervanes, or other objects which were considered essential to a good life. So the do-it-yourself movement, which now has reached such astounding proportions, had deep roots in the American way of life. Its present manifestation, interestingly enough, has developed from an entirely different set of circumstances and, in no small degree, in reaction against mass production, lack of which nurtured it in the early years.

Something vital to human happiness was lost when the machine edged out handicraftsmanship and when the assembly line limited individual participation in the shaping of an object to mere placement of a particular part. The old-time craftsman could watch what he was making grow to completion under his hand: the modern workman, familiar only with details, has little knowledge of the many intricate procedures that come before and that follow his own particular stint. The impersonal and fragmentary nature of such work has bred a longing for true creation that now prods literally millions of Americans to join hobby groups and community art centers.

During the past few years design freedom, assured by new, exciting materials has spurred craftsmen to throw off the yoke of the past and to create articles of utility that are as contemporary in spirit as they are sound in design. Knowledge thus gained has expanded the horizons of craftsmanship beyond the limitations of traditional methods. No longer confined to champlevé and cloisonné techniques of the traditional jeweler's art, enameling can be as freely handled and can yield as much creative satisfaction as any other branch of the fine arts. While it is true that a master of the medium must be experienced in all its phases —drawing, painting, metalry, ceramics, chemistry and glass making—it is possible to simplify techniques so that they afford even the beginner the thrill of creation and give him infinite satisfaction. Although it has taken me many years to achieve a suitable degree of simplicity in working methods, what I have learned can now be passed along directly to students and laymen in easy to follow, step-by-step instruction.

The art and practice of enameling can be as simple or as complicated as the individual may desire. It is possible to start in a small way and, as ability increases, to exchange a small, inexpensive furnace for a larger one. Most people, fortunately, have at least a rudimentary creativeness which is discovered and developed as they become interested in a rewarding craft. After a little experience with the medium they will find it pliable and useful, and in time will develop their own manner of working. Many high school students who have been introduced to the medium in their classes have found, in enameling, a craft that has promised a gainful future.

The therapeutic value of work in the crafts has long been recognized. Creative activity has great restorative value in the healing processes. Enameling, in its simplest applications, is among the most rewarding of crafts that are available to hospitals and convalescent institutions. It is ideal for the craft classes in summer camps and for hobby groups generally. In an era when relatively early retirement is becoming something of a problem it offers an absorbing outlet for the creative urge. It is becoming a favorite relaxation for business and professional people in search for purposeful diversion. Many doctors and dentists have found themselves predisposed to enameling through the practice of their own professions. The dental furnace, for instance, serves perfectly for the firing of jewelry.

The housewife who knows the possibilities of her stove, unconsciously has taken a first step toward firing; so with a small furnace she can make a variety of objects such as jewelry, buttons, ornaments, ash trays, cups and many things suitable for her home and for gifts. As she becomes more proficient she may even find a commercial demand for these products made in her own home. Ceramic companies, enamel artists and craftsmen, in this country, do an annual business of several million dollars and the market is increasing steadily.

Enameling has some noteworthy advantages over other crafts. A peculiar thrill comes to the beginner who finds that glass will melt to a flowing point in three short minutes. Unlike the potter, whose product in the process of firing is walled up in a kiln for twenty-four hours of anxious waiting, the enamelist watches excitedly over his piece during its three-minute firing and, after it cools, may make corrections or add more enamel, and finally subject the piece to three more minutes of intense heat.

Of course there is a difference between the creative craftsman and the unskilled hobbyist. The former creates his own shapes and designs, the latter usually copies them. The professional, also, is not bound by size; in his more adequately equipped workshop he can produce anything from jewelry to big architectural works such as large murals.

Within recent years my own articles on enameling, published in trade and fine arts magazines and listed in this book, have elicited such enthusiastic response from students and craftsmen that I have felt the urgency of sharing my knowledge more completely and to more people by means of a book on the subject. Such a book is especially needed because personal instruction is limited to a small number of qualified teachers. I trust that my book will lead many readers into the delights of this fascinating and very practical art-craft.

Edward Winter

WHAT IS ENAMEL?

The often misused word *enamel* has come to denote a number of things. It is used to describe any glossy varnish, resinous paints or lacquers of vegetable origin, as well as the coating found on milady's fingernails. In consequence, the casual observer fails to understand the difference between the true vitreous enamels and the numerous glossy substances which share a superficial resemblance.

Vitreous enamel, as the name implies, is a glass, whether transparent, opalescent, opaque, black, white or colored. When this glass is ground into powdered form, applied dry or in liquid state to metals, and fused to the base under an intense heat of 1500° F., it is known as *vitreous enamel.* A range composed of three hundred or so colors and tints are produced, comprising all the primary and secondary colors and an infinite variety of intermediate shades and tones.

Glass Comparisons.—If a windowpane or an old bottle is broken up and scattered over a piece of copper and fired at an intense heat, only a portion of the glass will adhere to the metal because this type of glass is high in flint and wasn't made for fusing onto metals. The *enamel glasses* made for metals are of the borosilicate and lead variety which fuse at a lower temperature.

Durability of Vitreous Enamels.—In Leonardo da Vinci's (1452-1519) notebook writings, *Comparisons of the Arts,* as arranged in English by Edward MacCurdy, he devoted considerable space to comparing the permanence of paintings to sculpture. "Painting," he writes, "surpassed all human works by reason of the subtle possibilities which it contains." The one advantage which sculpture has is that of offering greater resistance to time. Yet painting offers like resistance if it is done upon thick copper, covered with a white opaque enamel, then painted upon with enamel colors and fired at high temperatures. In degree of permanence, it then surpasses even sculpture. While sculpture in bronze is imperishable, this vitreous enamel painting upon copper is eternal.

Such permanence is witnessed in the many works of enameling art from the fifth century B.C. which are still perfectly preserved in European and American museums.

Bowls in assorted sizes with straight sides or with gradual flairs, both shallow and deep, make beautiful and functional one-of-a-kind pieces. The two small bowls at the top are in plain light blue; the others are in transparent pink and chartreuse with sgraffito line design appearing through the enamel's surface.

WHAT YOU NEED TO BEGIN WITH

The craft of enameling has become so popular today that the domestic suppliers of enamels can suggest and sell to the beginner all the necessary simple materials and equipment for his first efforts. In later pages the names of suppliers are given and a more complete list of tools and equipment needed for advanced work. But the beginner can manage with a very limited equipment, increasing it as he advances.

The materials for the beginner doing the simplest things can be purchased for twenty or twenty-five dollars. At first, one can fire small objects with a propane hand torch instead of a furnace which might come later. Small furnaces can be bought for as little as twenty-five or thirty dollars. They will accommodate jewelry, ash trays, and other small objects.

MAKING BOWLS AND ASH TRAYS

The simple and easy procedure of making small bowls and ash trays is demonstrated by the accompanying step-by-step photographs.

The materials you need are few: enamel 80-mesh grind; an 80-mesh sieve; gum tragacanth as an adhesive; a camel's-hair brush to apply the adhesive with; water, and a simple fixatif blower for spraying the gum and water. For the metal work one needs a planishing hammer, a steel stake, a vice, hard wood log, a file, fine steel wool and emery cloth. The sheet copper is cut and formed and then pickled in sulphuric acid. A trivet or firing support, a chrome firing screen and a small furnace are needed. More specific information regarding these tools, materials, and other equipment is given in another chapter. Involved or complicated equipment is not at all necessary for the beginner's work.

17

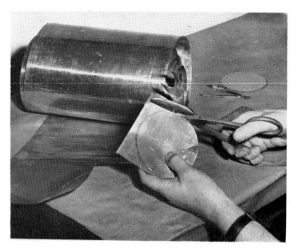

Cutting the circle from sheet copper with shears.

Hammering the flat disc into a cup-shaped hollow in the top of a hardwood log about 30 inches high. By pounding and revolving the disk, the metal rises into the shape of a bowl. The gouged-out cup shapes in the top of log need be no more than five or six inches in diameter. It can be gouged out with a wood carver's gouge and mallet.

Using a planishing hammer and iron stake, the bowl can be hammered into a cylindrical shape. The hammer marks are advantageous when a transparent enamel is fused over the surface. The planished surface produces interesting light reflections through the enamel.

The bottom of the bowl can be hammered in to make a suitable base.

Grinding down the edge of the bowl on a rubber-emery composition wheel.

Fine steel wool can be used to polish the surface of the metal.

"Pickling" the bowl in an acid-water solution.

Rinsing the bowl in clean water.

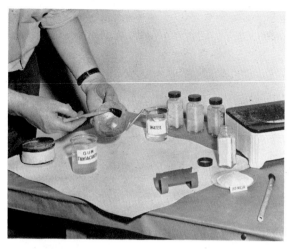

Coating the bowl with gum tragacanth and water solution.

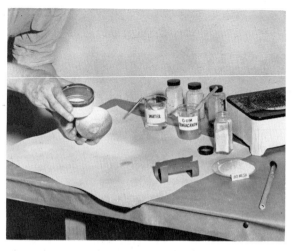

Sifting powdered enamel onto wet surface of bowl.

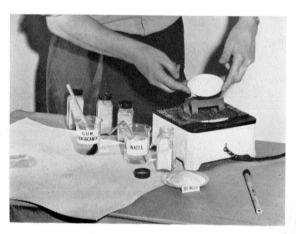

Drying the bowl over a hot plate.

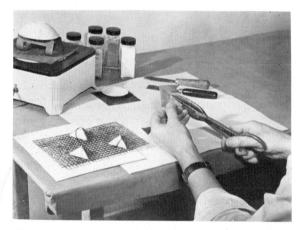

Simple tripods can be made by cutting one corner out of a square of nickel or chrome steel and bending the three sides together. These are then wired to the chromel planch with fine chromel wire, placing them according to the size of the piece.

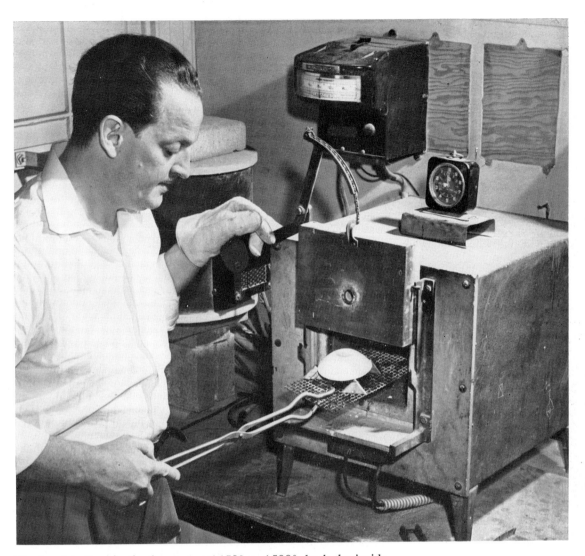

The bowl is fired in the furnace at 1450° to 1500°, both the inside and outside having been enameled. Any defects that may appear upon firing can be touched up and the piece re-fired.

This shows a 12-inch copper disk being shaped by the use of a
heavy stake.

The bowl is being planished over a steel stake (4″ diameter) by a half-round planishing hammer.

These hammered bowls are in a group of objects first to win a museum prize award in the United States (Cleveland Museum of Art) in 1933. The hammered bowl in the center is enameled in ruby red. The serving tray in the center is on a steel base. The one at the right shows transparent enamel applied over silver foil.

The start of a square ash tray. A small stake usually works better than a hammer for shaping a square. The cup-shaped depression in the log can be three or four inches in diameter.

Planishing bottom of tray on steel stake.

To give the piece a flat surface to rest on, it is placed on a steel plate and the base indented with a round hammer. If a ring foot is desired, the base need not be hammered in. *See* Footed Bowls.

STENCIL OR TEMPLATE METHOD

This is the simplified method of applying an enamel design either on the metal itself or over a previously fired enamel surface.

The drawing can be made directly on stencil paper or transferred onto it through carbon paper. A razor blade or X-acto knife can be used to cut out the design, which can be transferred to the metal by pouncing or dropping the enamel powder with a sieve through the open pattern of the stencil. The beginner should use an absorbent paper for stencils, inasmuch as this type of paper will absorb moisture from the water and gum tragacanth with which the metal is first coated and thus produce cleaner edges. Of course, the professional will use such masks as mere aids to the development of a design; he does not want the end result to look like a stencil. He will employ gradations and lose his edges here and there, thus achieving subtleties in his application of the enamel. Thus stencils, under the skilled hands of the enameler, offer unlimited possibilities for the imaginative, creative person.

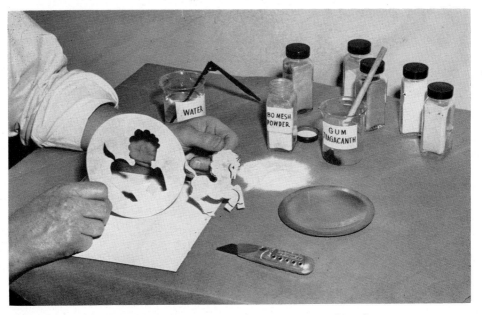

Template can be made by drawing the design on paper and cutting out the pattern with razor blade or sharp knife. Both the positive and negative areas of the design can be used.

The ash tray, having been shaped and thoroughly cleaned, is coated with a thin solution of gum tragacanth with a large camel's-hair brush. Care should be taken not to touch the surface of the metal that is to be enameled; oil from the skin will interfere with adherence of the enamel.

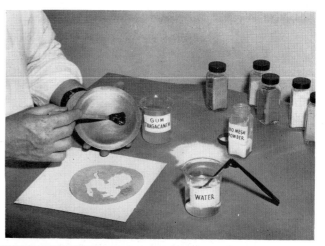

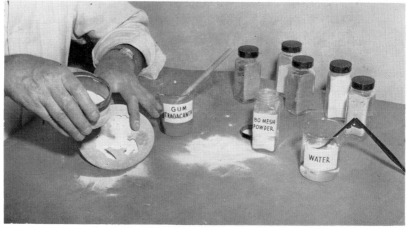

The open stencil should be placed on the copper and held tightly with the fingers while powdered enamel is sifted on. A tight edge will assure precise application of the design.

Before the stencil is lifted, a light spray of water, or water and gum solution, can be blown on to dampen the powdered enamel. The paper can then be removed.

26

Completed ash tray in brown, white and gold.

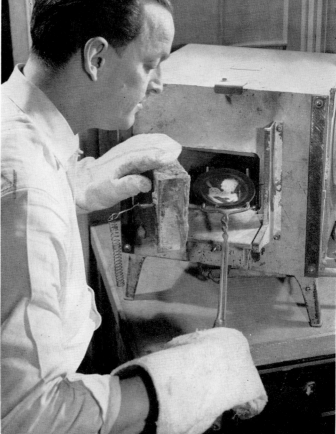

After the piece is dried out thoroughly on a hot plate or in an oven—twenty-five or thirty minutes—it is ready to be fired for a period of three minutes at a temperature of 1450° to 1500° F.

METALS USED FOR ENAMELING

The principal metals used for enameling are: copper, silver, steel, stainless steel, cast iron, gold, platinum, and aluminum.

It is possible to enamel many combinations of these metals wherein certain percentages of each metal are smelted together to produce an alloy.

Copper.—This metal is most commonly used for enameling. It is relatively soft and malleable and it stretches easily by hammering, spinning or raising. It can be purchased in sheets, rolls, bars, tubing, and wire from any number of suppliers or manufacturers, and it is relatively inexpensive. Beautiful transparent enamel surfaces can be produced over it.

If purchased in quantity, one can make an added saving. Sheets measuring 30 x 60 inches are common stock size. Copper also comes in rolls of 6, 8, 10, 12 and 20-inch widths in a variety of gauges. Copper 18 to 20 gauges is suitable for enameling, but the 18-gauge, being somewhat heavier, is preferred. This heavier copper can be fired many times in the furnace without warping out of shape, a distinct advantage over the 20-gauge.

When ordering, specify "cold rolled annealed." This copper has a good, smooth surface and is not likely to be pitted or contain scratches.

The 12-inch square plates, vase and small footed bowl by the author show a rather advanced use of the stencil, and illustrate the potential possibilities of this technique. The ruby plate, left, is in the collection of Mr. Rathbone Holme of London, England. The ruby vase is in the collection of Mrs. Benjamin P. Bole, Cleveland, Ohio. The yellow plate is in the collection of Mr. Syd Vickery, Wolverhampton, England.

Deep scratches in the copper must be polished with a buffer or fine steel wool before enameling; if not, they appear when the transparent enamel is fired. In storing sheets of copper, tissue paper should be kept between the sheets for protection.

Guilder's Metal.—This is a copper alloy containing 95% copper and 5% zinc, or 90% copper and 10% zinc. The beginner will do well to avoid it because it takes experience and skill to enamel it successfully. The higher the zinc content in copper, the more difficult it is to use. The 95% to 5% combination is used occasionally to produce ruby red enamels, but if one attempts to fire the piece two or three different times the enamel will tear and blister to a point of ruining the work. This blistering is caused by the zinc gases trying to escape through the hard enamel. If the piece can be completed with one or possibly two firings, the results will usually be satisfactory. Pink, lavender, and rose tones also can be produced with this metal. If blisters appear with too much firing the enamel can be hammered off and the piece re-enameled.

Silver.—Pure, or fine silver (0.295) can be enameled successfully. Best results are obtained by first firing a clear hard transparent flux (colorless enamel) over the metal. Enamels designed for application to silver are somewhat different in composition than those made for copper. Sheet or rolled silver may be ordered in similar gauges as copper. Transparent enamels on silver produce colors of a higher tonal key than on copper. It takes greater skill to enamel fine silver; the metal is harder and, if warping appears in the piece in firing, it is harder to get rid of before the piece cools. And since the cost is considerably higher, mistakes are much more costly.

Sterling Silver.—This is an alloy of silver that contains 92½% of silver and 7½% copper. It presents the same difficulty in enameling as the guilder's metal; successive firings result in blisters and cracks. German silver cannot be enameled due to its composition of 60% copper, 20% nickel, and 20% zinc.

Gold.—Gold was a popular metal with Renaissance enamelists, but because of its exorbitant cost pure gold is scarcely used today. Anyway, it is difficult to enamel because of its softness in its pure state.

However, red gold (50% gold, 50% copper) can be enameled as can green gold (50% gold, 50% silver). And twenty-four carat gold that has been beaten into a thin foil, leaf or paillons can be very successfully enameled. It is in this form that gold will find increasing use.

Platinum.—Platinized silver, an alloy comprising 95 parts of silver and 5 parts of platinum, is sometimes used for costume jewelry; in its pure state it is impractical for enameling because the enamel will not adhere to it successfully. Since platinum has a terrific rate of expansion, it is incompatible with the expansion of the enamel. However, platinum, in liquid form, can be painted onto an enamel surface and fired successfully. Overfiring will cause it to fade out and disappear.

Bronze.—Attempts to enamel this alloy of copper (90% copper and 10% tin) frequently present considerable difficulties because tin boils under intense heat. But extremely heavy gauges of bronze will be more likely to accept enamel successfully.

Brass.—Common brass is a copper-zinc alloy containing one third zinc and two thirds copper. Due to this high zinc content, brass sheet-

The Wine Bottle. Enamel on a 16-inch copper bowl in blue, lavender, green-white with transparent colors over silver foil. White crackle enhances the textural quality. An example of the template process using silver foil. Owned by Mr. and Mrs. Joseph W. Fribley, Shaker Heights, Ohio, 1936.

ing or plate is not suitable for enameling. The boiling of the zinc under intense heat will cause the enamel to pop off.

Steel, Iron, and *Aluminum.*—These metals are discussed in other chapters.

This 4 x 5½-foot *Angel Fish* panel, produced by the template method, is the first vitreous enameled steel mural ever produced. The design is in blue, turquoise, yellow green, brown and white. Collection of Robert A. Weaver, Chairman of Board of Ferro Corporation, Cleveland, Ohio.

Costume Jewelry. Brooches, in assorted opaque and transparent colors, stylized designs. All have solid silver and brass sheet backs with bezeled edges overlapping the enamel, giving a professional quality to the work. Using polished metal backing no counter-enamel surface or sharp edges are exposed. Bottom section: Transparent and opaque enamel on copper and silver. Cuff links, needles for brooches, and ear wires.

JEWELRY

The adornment of mankind with precious stones, metals and jewel enamels had its origin in the earliest days of history. Fired, colored enamels became substitutes for precious gems; but it was not a case of imitation as the art of enameling became great in its own right. The massive crown jewels of state, and the sacred ornaments of religion, the wedding band, and utilitarian buckled pins and buttons for clothing were but a few of the forms taken by the jeweler's art. Today enameled jewelry is a fine art and an exciting craft that is well within the abilities of the student craftsman.

Although it is not our intention to treat jewelry extensively in this book—there are many excellent works exclusively devoted to this subject*—the accompanying demonstrations will suffice for the beginner. Many artists have been introduced to the art of enameling through their first efforts in jewelry work; their enthusiasm in this craft leading them on to larger bowl, mural, and painting projects.

Jewelry appeals to amateurs because small, decorative objects can be made with limited and inexpensive firing equipment in small furnaces, and because of the relatively short length of time required to complete such simple pieces as pins and brooches.

A knowledge of small space breaking, color pattern, and designing for any given shape is all-important before one undertakes the techniques of enamel application and firing. Along with the design of an article, one must remember that jewelry, as a personal ornament, must integrate itself with the costume as a whole and be complimentary and flattering to the wearer.

It is best for the student to have learned something about working with metals, cutting, filing, soldering and polishing before he takes on the addition of colored enamels.

For a brooch or pin to be professionally correct, the piece of enamel

---

*A most valuable treatise for the student of jewelry making is *Jewelry Making as an Art Expression* by D. Kenneth Winebrenner. This is an exhaustive work on the subject and will prove stimulating to the enameler.

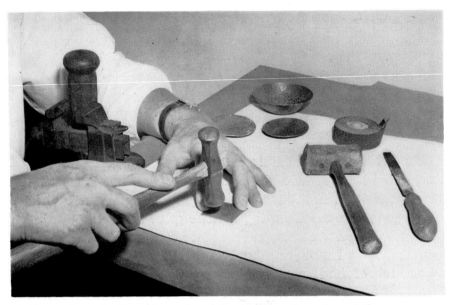

Making a brooch. By using a hard flat surface, the edge of the square can be straightened evenly on all four sides.

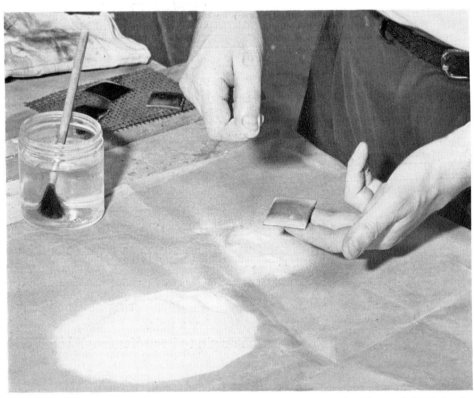

After the cleaning and pickling process, already explained in the text, and after brushing a thin solution of water and gum traga-canth on the metal to receive and hold the powdered enamel, the enamel is applied through the fingers evenly or dusted on through a small sieve.

34

GROUPS OF ENAMELS DESIGNED BY THELMA FRAZIER WINTER, 1955

Students applying enamel to pins and brooches.

Cuff links, enamel on copper; designed and executed by Thelma Frazier Winter.

should be set into a flat piece of silver, brass, or aluminum with a bezel turned back over the enamel, as in a setting for a stone. The metal backing and the edge can then be highly polished. The needle itself can be of silver soldered to the metal backing. The color range is wide; there are dozens of transparent as well as opaque enamels for all metals. Ground to approximately 80-mesh by the supplier (or by the craftsman himself), the processes of application are exactly the same as in making ash trays, bowls, and plaques. Working on small pieces of metal requires just as much handling skill as that of producing larger utilitarian objects. Transparent enamels produce colors of higher key on pure silver than on copper which has a warmer base. Opaque enamel, of course, will completely cover any base metal, and interesting designs (abstract, conventional and realistic) can be produced with them.

Eight brooches and cuff links are enameled at one time by placing them on a chrome wire screen for fusing in the furnace for two to three minutes at 1500° F. White strings of enamels were used for textures on these pieces.

37

With a felt buffer and rouge the cuff link back can be highly polished. With a camel's-hair brush, coat the polished metal with hard lacquer to preserve its brightness indefinitely.

A propane hand torch is used to solder the cuff link backs onto the metal with a soft easy-flowing solder. Some backs come from the supplier with small particles of solder already attached to the piece for easy fusing. The propane hand torch, applied underneath, fuses the enamel easily within three or four minutes. By experience, one learns to gauge the proper distance of flame from the piece. When lumps of frit or other speckled textures are used, the torch can be played downward onto the piece. The hand torch is effective because the operator can control the firing readily. It is exciting to watch the enamel fuse and take on a glossy surface.

Enameled ring greatly enlarged. Small enamels can be set into a silver ring bezel—this one is rectangular. By tightly fitting the enamel into it and hammering the thin silver bezel over its edges, the rough edges of the enamel are completely covered. Great care must be taken to avoid fracturing the enamel in hammering. The bezel and entire ring can then be highly polished.

METALRY

The professional enamelist must know all phases of the metalworking art: raising, forming, planishing, soldering, cleaning, etching, sawing and cutting. With this knowledge and skill in applying it, he is not dependent upon or confined to preformed or mass-produced, stock metal items. Moreover, hand-hammered pieces naturally bring higher prices. Metals that have been raised by hand, beautifully planished and perfected in all details of finish, produce a more luminous and transparent effect when enameled than plain machine-polished metal surfaces do. But, of course, a hand-hammered ash tray or bowl is in no need of an opaque enamel design that would cover the beautiful hammered surface.

Workshop equipment and tools are naturally of first consideration in any craft work, but often much can be done with a very limited number of tools to start with; these may be supplemented from time to time. The more skilled one is with small hand tools—chasing tools, dapping punches, scorpers, and other engraving tools and hammers—the more resourceful he will be in treating the metal with exciting designs to produce unique work.

There are a number of toolmakers who specialize in every tool for metalcraft and they have illustrated catalogues which will be found helpful in choosing any type of tool. The beginner can practically set himself up with most of this equipment by a visit to his nearest hardware store. Planishing hammers, stakes, metal, and enamel are the few items that would have to be ordered from tool and enameling manufacturers. There are books on metalworking that can also be valuable.

TOOLS AND MATERIALS

The professional metal craftsman has a great interest in and love for a variety of tools, and they all serve their purpose in enabling him to turn out skilled work. The metalworking and enameling tools pictured here were chosen with the beginner and student in mind.

Although much of the author's work reproduced here—jewelry, bowls, plaques, vases, and murals — is executed in what might be termed as "painter's" technique, the entire surface of the metal being covered with enamel, he emphasizes that there is an extensive field of creative enameling that can be developed by emphasizing decorative treatments of the surface of the metal itself such as chasing, texturing the metal with assorted punches and hammers, and the greater use of designs developed by use of acids. Work of a new character, style, design, and feeling would then be developed and repoussé and champlevé processes would be exceedingly popular. A combination of both opaque as well as transparent enamels could be applied to the etched metal surface to produce startling effects.

REPOUSSÉ OR CHASING

Chasing is a means of decorating metalwork by patterns beaten into it, with special tools, either on the face or on the reverse side; the pattern in the first case will be depressed; in the second, raised. Repoussé, as chasing work is often called, is an art which was mastered by metal craftsmen in early history. It has sometimes been referred to as sculpture in metal as it gives the flat surface of sheet metal a three-dimensional effect.

Chasing tools come in various sizes and shapes. With practice one soon learns what they will and won't do. The metal to be given the tooled design is placed in chaser's pitch. The pitch can be held in a spherical pitch block or suitable metal bowl.

The student should begin with a very simple design for most work using 20 or 22-gauge copper or silver. By applying a torch or flame to the pitch it will soften and the metal can be seated in it. When the pitch cools to room temperature, it hardens and gives a firm, cushioning base for the metal. It is often necessary to anneal the metal to make it soft and pliable for working. This can be done with a torch or by placing the metal in the enameling furnace for a minute and a half or until it gets red hot. In order to avoid gouging or scratching it, use round and oval planishing tools rather than a chisel-edge tool.

ETCHING

Etching is the process of removing metal by chemical means in order to produce a surface design. Those portions of the designs which are to be eaten away are left exposed to the action of the acid, while all other surfaces are covered with an acid-resist asphaltum which protects them from the acid. The success in etching a design on metal depends a great deal on the preparation of clean metal and the care taken in painting on the design.

The procedure is as follows: 1. Trace or draw the design full size on a piece of paper. 2. Clean metal surface with fine steel wool or a clean rag and alcohol. 3. Paint surface with whiting (1 part whiting, 5 parts water, 5 parts alcohol, a few drops of liquid soap). 4. When whiting is dry, transfer the design to the metal, using carbon paper.

Assorted chasing tools. Made of hard tool steel they are ideal for repoussé work on all metals. They are square-shaped with rounded edges and polished ends.

Tools for background decorating may be purchased individually or in sets. Impressions are made on any metal to be enameled by striking the tool with a hammer. Design patterns thus made show clearly through any flux or transparent metal. Ideal for bracelets, earrings, brooches or allover patterns on ash trays.

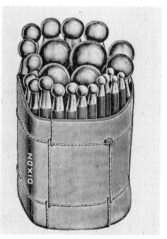

Above: Iron dapping dies; sizes 1¾, 2¼, 2¾ and 3 inches. The many concave depressions in these dies will shape thin, flat metal into rounded contours of various sizes with the aid of dapping punches. Rounded metal disks, after enameling, can become sections of bracelets and other jewelry forms.

Dapping punches in assorted sizes making a complete set consisting of 12, 18, 24 or 30 to each set.

Left: Here the craftsman is executing a design in relief by hammering a smooth, rounded chasing tool on a copper piece. The metal has been set in chaser's pitch, which was heated with a torch to soften it so that the metal is held fast when the pitch cools and hardens. The piece is removed when chased, by again heating the pitch.

41

5. With a fine scratch awl, scratch the design into the metal. 6. Wash off the whiting and clean both sides of the metal with fine steel wool. Avoid handling surfaces which have been cleaned. 7. Lay the face of the piece on clean paper and paint the back and edges of the metal with black asphaltum varnish, covering it completely. 8. After back is dry, turn over and paint all surfaces of the design which are to be protected from the acid and remain in relief after etching. The asphaltum should be allowed to dry for six or eight hours. 9. Mix up etching solution in a Pyrex glass dish or other suitable container that is not metal, using 3 parts water and 1 part nitric acid for copper and silver and 3 parts water and 1 part hydrochloric acid for aluminum. In order to avoid burning the hands, *always add the acid to the water*. Pouring water on the acid will generate steam and is dangerous. 10. The length of time for etching depends upon the strength of the acid, the temperature of the acid bath, and the depth etch that is desired. If bubbles develop during the etching process, they can be wiped away by the use of a feather or a cotton swab. If any of the asphaltum chips off in the process, spots can be retouched with a brush and placed back in the acid. 11. Rinse in clean water when completed and remove asphaltum with turpentine or lacquer thinner. 12. Scrub with pumice powder and brush and rinse. 13. Piece is ready to enamel.

BASSE-TAILLE (Bahss-tah-ee)

This is the traditional name given to metal surfaces that are etched, engraved or chased and then enameled. After engraving or etching, and after the metal is cleaned, it should be given a light coating of transparent flux or clear, colored enamel. The enamel will naturally appear darker in the lower parts of the design where it settles, and the high areas will be lighter in key. Melted enamel on such a metal surface sometimes gives a fine, third-dimensional, sculptured effect. Traditionally, this technique was popular in making dresser sets, bracelets, vanity objects and jewelry; it offers a great challenge to today's enamelers and has creative possibilities far beyond those available to its practitioners of past generations.

Opposite Page: Examples of metal surfaces textured by chasing—concave, convex and crosshatching; etching, engraving and by masking-off and rubbing with fine steel wool to make unusual grounds on which to apply and fuse opaque and transparent enamels. Large and small hammers and small steel chasing tools are used for repoussé on all kinds of metals.

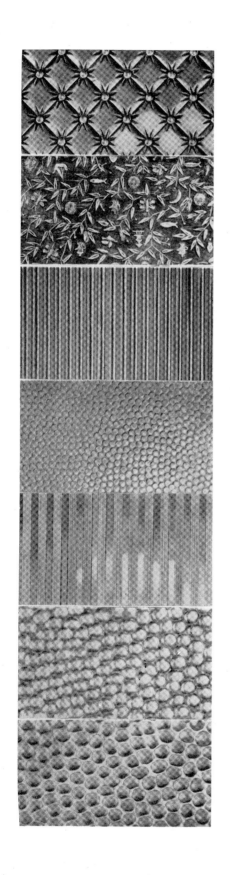

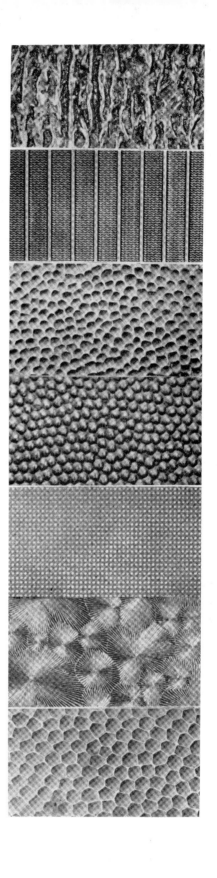

FROM SHEET COPPER TO FINISHED ENAMEL

1. Crinkle-edged bowl is hand-raised and planished from a round disk of 18-gauge copper. The raising operation is done in hollow of hard wood log. If foot is desired a copper ring can be silver-soldered to bowl before firing.

2. A straight-sided bowl can be hammered the same way or spun over a wood chuck on a lathe. The gold decoration is applied and fired after the enamel is fired.

3. The 3½-inch ash tray is hammered and formed in the same way.

4. Kitchen match holder is fashioned from sheet of 18-gauge copper. Mark out proper proportions with pencil and then chisel-edge-cut these lines so that the edges will break with an even corner. All sides may be enameled, or just the top.

5. Small match safe may be made the same way.

6. Small match safe with domed and planished top. The doming should be done when the metal is in flat shape, then bend the edges. Transparent enamel shows more luminous on hand-hammered surface.

7. Domed copper square for compact insert. Doming is done on top of a log as in #1.

8. Brooch can be made using flat piece of copper or by doming it and then enameling.

9. Small flat ash tray can be made from a 3-inch circle of sheet copper.

44

CEDAR-LINED BRASS CIGARETTE BOX WITH COPPER-HINGE TOP

1. Cut paper pattern the size of the box. Using 20-gauge brass, copper, or silver, lay paper pattern accurately over the metal. Then cut out corners with tinning shears.

2. Thin cedar wood inlay. Five pieces cut accurately to fit into metal box; all corners must be beveled to fit tight. The bottom is cut to fit the entire bottom of box and is placed in first. The ends and sides are then fitted in.

3. The four corners of the metal box must be mitered and filed accurately, then tied around tight with thin metal wire to hold in place while each corner is soldered individually with hard silver solder. If the box is not to be enameled, but polished and lacquered, an easy-flow soft solder can be used.

4. Small copper tubing to be used for the hinge can be purchased from a metal supplier and soldered to the copper box top with *hard* silver solder, as soft solder will not stand up in the heat of the furnace. Three portions of the same sized tubing are soldered onto the metal box so that the top of the tubing is flush with the top of the box. Medium hard solder is satisfactory, providing the box is not to be enameled.

5. The edge of the top is turned down with a notch filed out of both of the edges where the copper round wire is to be placed through the tubing to make the hinge adhere to the top of the box. Enameling process for the top is the same as for trays and bowls. After the top has been enameled and fired, the edge is stoned-off and polished on a buffer. The top is placed onto the box and untempered copper wire cut to size and run through the tube hinge.

45

Cigarette boxes, variety ash receivers, brooches, pins, and compacts illustrating a variety of ways colorful enamel and assorted textures can be effectively made; all on a copper base.

Forming cover for large metal matchbox, using straight, flat-edge form and hammering with a rawhide mallet.

These footed bowls by the author vary from 5 to 12 inches in diameter. Plain, transparent colors, speckled edges and crackles add to the individuality and uniqueness of each piece.

FOOTED BOWLS

Footed bowls are much more difficult to enamel than plain shapes. Using a ring foot one must be proficient in soldering, cleaning, and pickling both the foot and the bowl. And they have to be securely tied together with wire to assure successful flow of the solder. After the soldering has been done, the piece must again be cleaned and pickled preparatory to applying the enamel. This type of enameling belongs to an advanced course, due to the fact that the student has the inside and outside of the foot, as well as the inside and outside of the bowl, to apply the powdered enamel to. With great exactness and careful manipulation, all sides (inside and outside) can be enameled at one time and the piece fired. A water and gum tragacanth spray to dampen it will make this operation easier, but once the entire bowl is enameled great care must be taken in drying so that none of the powder will fall off from the back sides. If a portion of the enamel does fall while drying, it is best to complete the firing process and patch up the error with the next firing. All burned off or oxidized areas must be cleaned before enamel is applied to these spots. Brass rings can be used for the base of a bowl and, while brass will not enamel, the bowl itself can be enameled and the brass ring polished and lacquered as the last operation.

47

The most difficult task for the enameler is to apply enamel successfully and fuse it to the deep sides of a vase or other cylindrical shapes where the walls are perpendicular. Having mastered footed bowls, the problem of making a vase will be much easier. The use of water and gum spraying to dampen the powdered surface will assure a successful bond to the copper. Care must be taken in handling the piece in drying as well as firing to produce a perfect enameling job. Transparent enamels flowing down the deep sides of a vase will produce a highly transparent and beautiful surface. Special pronged firing tools must be used to hang the vase on while firing and a deep furnace firing chamber is necessary to receive the piece adequately. When the tall vase comes from the furnace, it can be grabbed with asbestos gloves and turned upside down on a flat surface to straighten the edge of the vase and produce a perfect, round surface.

The bowl and ring foot must have been cleaned previously and pickled in acid before soldering which cannot be done on dirty or greasy surfaces.

The copper-ring foot should be centered on the base of the bowl and tied tightly with fine steel wire to hold it firmly for the hard silver soldering operation, which can also be done in the enameling furnace.

Deep-sided vases like these are the most difficult to execute. The powdered enamel is inclined to drop off the sides in the process of drying and firing. Specially designed firing pins must be used to hold the top rim of the vases for successful firing and a large and deep muffle furnace is required. The vases are made of 18-gauge copper by the spinning method. An easier way of firing is to leave the enamel off on the bottom so that the piece can be fired in an upright position on a planch.

FREE FORM

Free form, or the designing of asymmetric shapes in metal, can be exciting for the craftsman who wants to get away from the circular, square or oblong shapes. Many free forms are derived from similar forms in nature. In going back to nature the craftsman's horizon widens and his work becomes more imaginative. Of course, the applied design in enamel for a free form must conform to the given shape of the metal.

Cutting free-form shapes out of metal with tinning shears makes a fine problem for the metal craftsman; the operation of shaping, planishing and forming by hand will produce unique pieces. If ringed bases are used, they must conform to the general contour of the bowl.

A simple Limoges method; painting the pattern on the previously fired, white enameled vase—a section of copper tubing—with a finely ground black painter's enamel. It can be "flash fired," put in and out of the furnace rapidly to burn away oils before it is entered into the furnace for permanent fusing at 1450° F. Tubing in assorted lengths is available for use as lamp bases.

This is a kind of enameling technique that is of interest to painters. The name is taken from the town of Limoges, France, the home of masters who created this specialized form of painter's enamel. In the Limoges technique, finely ground enamels are painted with a brush on a previously fired enamel surface of most any color, transparent or opaque surface.

Limoges artists handled all kinds of subject matter, including portraits, allegorical scenes, ornaments, figure compositions, and landscapes. All types of brushes, narrow, wide or pointed were used to apply the enamel. All artists had their own particular style and technique of handling.

Most of the author's enamel art pieces reproduced in this book might be described as Limoges or some variation of the painter's approach to the medium, though many panels and bowls have been executed with combinations of techniques, such as template, line drawing, sgraffito, inlay or crackle. It is the end result that is important, regardless of the processes and techniques used.

A complete knowledge of the medium is necessary and the artist must fully acquaint himself with its full range of possibilities as well as its limitations if he intends to exploit it to the fullest. However, it is a medium that is very inviting to any resourceful painter and relatively easy to master. He will experience a thrill in working with permanent, vitreous pigments as his paints, subjected to a 1450° F. intense heat, come forth in a new dimension of color and texture. He can express his personal style of painting in this medium whether in portraits, landscapes or any other kind of subject matter. At his command is a full range of finely ground enamels to satisfy his own color predilections.

Enamel for the painting technique must be very finely ground, approximately 250 to 400- mesh, approximately the same fineness as that of face powder. It is then mixed with pine oil for body and either alcohol or pure gum turpentine is used for a thinner. These ingredients can be worked into the proper painting consistency with a palette knife on a glass slab. The painting can be done on opaque white, gray, black or any other colored fired enamel. An opaque surface, being relatively stationary, is usually preferred to a transparent one, which has a tendency to flow slightly when being fired.

If an assortment of colors is desired, they can be mixed and kept in a small porcelain jar which should be covered to keep them free from dirt and dust and any foreign matter. Before any ambitious painting is

Carnival. An opaque enamel on a 10 x 30-inch steel panel in a technique that combines painting, drawing, and sgraffito. The colors are lavender, white, gold, and black. Collection The Cleveland Museum of Art, 1953.

attempted, it is advisable to make test samples of colors, tonal effects, and gradations and note any undesirable results that may appear under successive firings. In working with these colors one should fire the enamels approximately two to three minutes from 1350° F. to 1450° F. If five or six firings are required to complete the work, this time can be cut down to two minutes or under for each because of the several separate firings.

One must always remember that before placing the painting in the intense heat of the furnace, the volatile or organic medium used to thin the enamel and give it body must be burned away by holding it at the open door of the furnace until the oils have stopped smoking.

As has been said, this is an ideal medium for painters experienced in oil or watercolor who are attracted by its exciting possibilities. Those who might ask how they can fire their work or have it fired, should be assured that almost any commercial enamel manufacturer—and there are many throughout the country—will gladly arrange for the use of their furnaces for a nominal charge.

However, there are smaller furnaces available for purchase, ranging in size and price from twenty-five dollars up. It has been the experience of many artists that the smaller furnaces with which they started working can be sold to others, and that they can acquire larger equipment as their ambition develops and their market increases. The painter who begins with small panels which are appropriate for framing in home decoration is likely to discover a market opening up for larger work.

Even with a relatively small furnace more ambitious work can be done by the assembling of individual units into a larger design area as seen in examples illustrated on following pages. The architectural field in itself offers great opportunity for enamel; there is an increasing acceptance by architects of this beautiful permanent medium.

I wish to emphasize the fact that painting with enamels is not such a foreign technique as it might at first seem to a painter accustomed to working on canvas or board. A still life, landscape, or figure composition

Calla Lily. A 30 x 30-inch opaque enamel panel on steel base. The colors are brown, blue green, white and black. Silver foil was used in the butterfly wings. Collection The Cleveland Museum of Art, 1940.

Plantation. Using painter's enamel technique on a single sheet of 18-gauge copper, 30 x 60 inches, in transparent and opaque enamels. The colors are blue green, yellow green, black, and white.

Twenty-two-inch floral plaque in yellow, brown, dark green, black, and white; brown and gold vase; emerald green covered bowl and tray; chartreuse hand-hammered square dish. All are on 18-gauge copper.

Annunciation. Enamel in Limoges technique in copper 24 x 24 inches. Grayed yellow, light blue, dark blue, and black. Collection Miss Lucia McBride, New York City, 1940.

Harvest. A vitreous enamel mural using six 2-foot square sections of flanged 18-gauge steel 4 x 6 feet. Yellow, brown, red, green, gray, and dark green and black edge. Collection International Business Machines, Endicott, New York, 1942.

can be done in the artist's own studio and taken to the closest enameling furnace available for firing. For corrections or additions to a design the piece can again be taken to the furnace for another firing. The painted panels will not be damaged (through enamel dropping off) in transportation, since the kind of enamel paint used adheres firmly to the enamel surface.

TEXTURES

The possibilities inherent in the use of textures, unknown to traditional enamelists, have played an important part in attracting the interest of students and artists. Having had the advantage of working in a plant where the process of enamel making was going on from the raw materials to the finished glass frit, I have had the opportunity of making my own opaque and transparent batches of enamel. The heavy and thin enamel strings that are now so popular I developed from the drippings of enamel in its molten state; also glass lumps, balls, and half-domed shapes made from droplets of melted enamel. In visiting glass factories and suppliers I have experimented with colored glass balls, beads, and rods. If these are not too large or heavy, many interesting effects can be produced with them.

Texture means character of surface—smooth, rough, coarse, fine, hard or soft; it is the tactile quality of surface that can contribute much to the visual variety of your work. Textures add subtleties and variations to surface, thereby relieving monotony. They can be used to dramatize subject matter, whether realistic or abstract; but the abstractionist can probably best profit by them. Third-dimensional effects can be achieved by using strings, lumps, balls, beads, copper wire, silver, gold and white

Enamel on steel panel 24 inches square. Colors: Black, red, white, and green. White strings and gold threads are used to give texture.

57

threads, hair threads, metal foil, even small wheels and springs taken from watches, and many more materials that are not combustible.

Most textural materials are applied to the enamel surface when the work is near the completed state; if applied during the first two or three firings, they will be completely melted down during successive firings and thus kill the raised effect that is so desired. The beginner playing with textures in a careless or haphazard manner can produce some horrible results. One must learn to be selective and apply the same principles in the use of texture as one would to color, drawing, composition, and design in any medium. By subtle and skilled arrangements of dull, mat or opaque surfaces, the transparent surface becomes even more luminous in depth. Enamels are perfect naturals for textural effects in that they can be used in any degree of fusion or grind, from fritted lumps half an inch or more in diameter to the fineness of 400-mesh. Strings can also be produced from one-quarter or one-half-inch strands to the fineness of a hair. Whenever using heavy textures, the base metal on which they are applied should be of heavy weight, usually sixteen to eighteen gauge. When the thickness and weight of enamel exceeds that of the metal itself, there will be trouble, due to varying expansion and contraction of metal and enamel. While many of my developments such as strings and crackle effects made from liquid slip or slush enamel are available on the market, it behooves the craftsman to use textural effects with intelligent restraint.

TYPES OF MATERIAL USED TO CREATE TEXTURED SURFACES
Fine silver wire; sharply pointed steel tools; lumps and strings of enamel; small transparent glass balls; pocket comb.

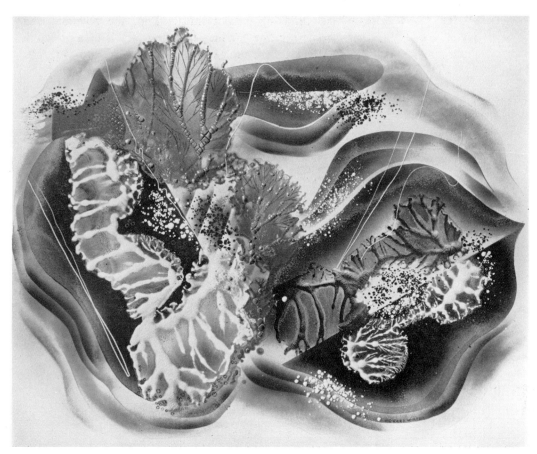

Metamorphosis. This shows how strings (the very thin white lines) and frit (the assorted-sized lumps) have been used to add textural beauty to an enameled panel. Collection The Cleveland Museum of Art, 1947.

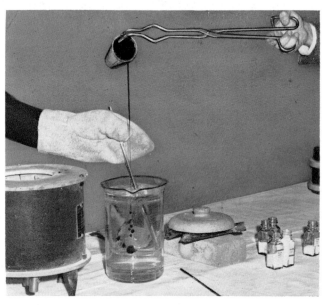

This is a simplified process of making enamel frit from raw materials by fusing the raw materials in an electric pot smelter (Hoskin's Pot Smelter #PD-104, Volts 110, Amps 10.9). The liquid enamel is poured into a beaker of water and in the stirring process breaks up into lumps of frit.

Making a "pot smelt." Pour the raw materials from the bag into crucible which is then placed in a round, drum-shaped heating unit shown below. Transparent enamel, made in this manner, is removed from the pot smelt and poured out to cool on large slabs of steel.

Opaque white strings of enamel are formed by dipping a steel rod into the liquid enamel and letting it drip onto a concrete floor or asbestos sheeting. Strings produced in this manner are used for textures such as those seen on pages 57, 59 and 61.

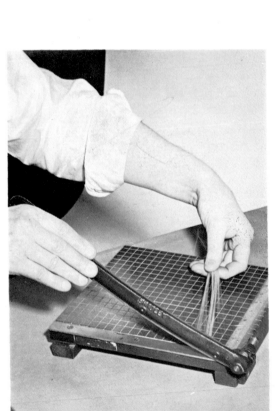

Gold hair-threads (24-carat) are cut into desired lengths with a sharp paper cutter. They produce a very fine gold line when fired into an enamel surface.

This shows an assortment of fired-string textures of varied widths ready for use.

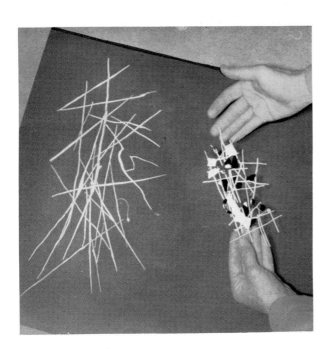

White string textures fused together in an abstract pattern. Opaque black and red frit used for accents. Interesting filigree can be devised. Sections can be lightly fused together with the hand torch. The parts are laid on an asbestos sheet and lightly heated with a torch so that they partially fuse ready for application to any enameled surface.

Decorative objects in transparent, emerald green on copper illustrating how string textures and lumps, used with restraint, make effective decorative treatments. The green enamel is fused before the strings are applied and fired.

Silver Birches. Opaque enamel on 25 x 30-inch steel. White string textures combined with lumps of white and red frit. Sgraffito is used to make cross-hatched lines. Colors are gray, olive green, yellow, black, and red, 1948.

Metropolis. Opaque enamel on 30 x 35-inch steel panel. Textures are made with lumps of frit, strings, a pocket comb. The colors are gray, white, black, and red. Collection Dr. T. B. R. Webster, New York City, 1949.

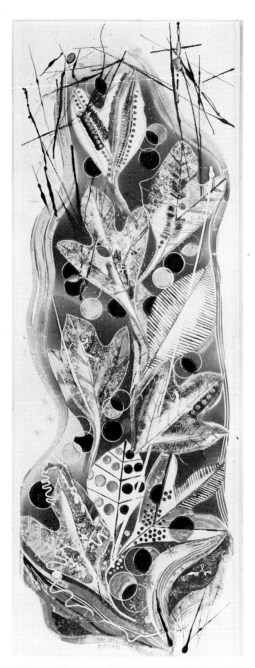

Autumn Leaves. Opaque enamel 12 x 28-inch steel. Black and white string textures were generously used to give tactile quality to surface. Liquid gold and platinum give quality to leaves. A drawing compass was used to make white line circles. Collection The Cleveland Museum of Art, 1953.

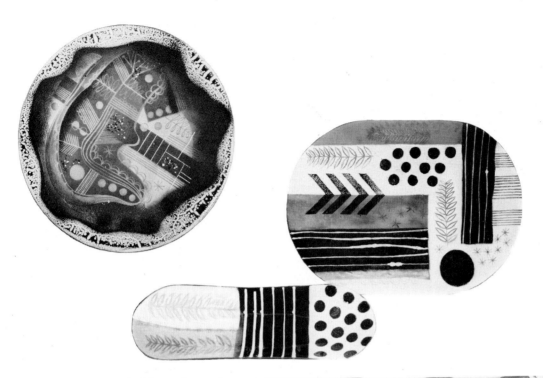

The two oval objects above show another interesting use of textures. The dots and chevrons were achieved through the use of stencils. The round plaque (18 inches in diameter), in sgraffito, is in the collection of the New York State College of Ceramics, Alfred, New York.

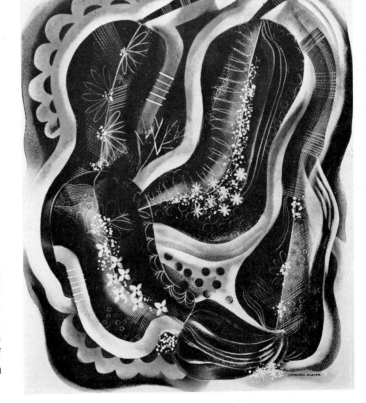

Gourds. Opaque and transparent enamel in a 30 x 35-inch steel panel. The colors are chartreuse, gray, brown, black, and gold. Note use of sgraffito and lumps of frit for accents. Collection of the Butler Institute of American Art, Youngstown, Ohio.

Transfiguration. An opaque and transparent enamel on a 24-inch square steel panel. A pocket comb was used to give white line graining effect. Syracuse Museum of Fine Art, 1940.

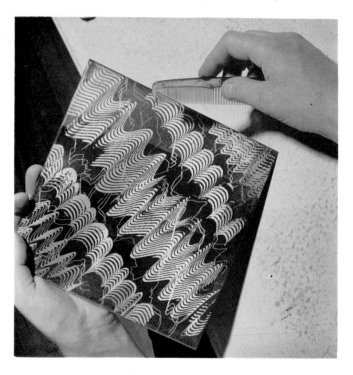

Using a previously fired light or dark enamel surface, interesting designs and line drawings can be made by combing with an ordinary pocket comb. A 200-mesh, black enamel was applied to the light surface and dampened with a spray of gun tragacanth and water and then dried to prevent tearing of the enameled surface during the combing. To produce black lines, use a white enamel over a previously fired black surface.

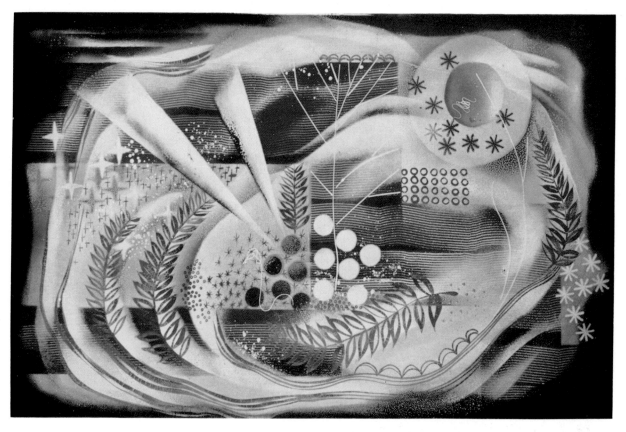

Summer. The comb technique was used in the design of this 20 x 35-inch opaque enamel on steel. The colors are yellow, blue green, brown, and white; white strings and lumps of white and black frit have been used. Collection of Mr. and Mrs. Thomas E. Thompson, Highland Park, Ill.

Fruit Composition. Opaque and transparent enamel on a 24-inch square steel panel. Textural effects acquired by use of solid 1/32-inch glass balls and white strings. Collection of Syracuse Museum of Fine Arts, Syracuse, N. Y., 1941.

TILES, SECTIONALS, MOSAICS

Tiles made in square or oblong shapes varying in size from an inch or even less up to the common six, eight or ten-inch variety, offer great possibilities as decorative, colorful inserts in table tops, mirror frames, lamp bases, wall decorations and cigarette boxes. As a matter of fact, they can be made almost any size, as elements of sectional murals, given a suitable furnace for firing large work. No matter what their size, the individual pieces can be sunk into a stone, brick or cement wall to produce colorful, textured designs. Very small metal enamel squares can be fused with a propane hand torch and larger sections attempted depending upon the size of the furnace or firing muffle.

For table tops or trays, any suitable piece of thin plywood will serve as a base to hold the pieces. Regular tile setting cement, black miracle adhesive, or any other rubber-base compound can be used to make the mosaic pieces adhere to the plywood. White or colored tile filler powder, mixed with a little water can then be poured over the tiles to fill the joints. Rubbing with a damp cloth will remove the excess filler.

Metal tiles must receive the same cleaning and pickling process given to bowls and ash trays, and the enamel application also follows the same procedure. All types of sgraffito, painting, inlay, stencil, and brush-and-rubber-roller techniques can be used to decorate the tiles. Liquid gold, silver, platinum and other lusters are also useful in adding quality of surface.

Right: The corners of an 18-gauge piece of copper are cut so that the four sides can be bent down on the pencil lines.

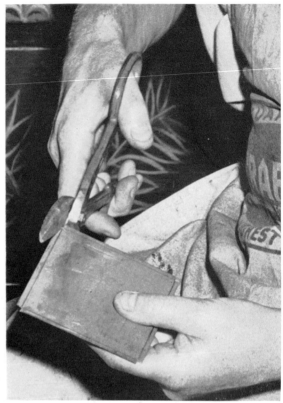

Left: Use a hammer to bend the sides over tool steel edge. The corners should be soldered on the underside with hard silver solder in order to keep them together during successive firings. For cleaning, polishing, and pickling, follow directions given in the demonstration of making an ash tray.

After the copper tile has been cleaned and pickled, it should be rinsed in clean water and dried. It is then dipped into an opaque enamel solution of any colored slip, sometimes referred to as slush. Hold by the edge and cover both sides completely. One or two brisk shakes will dislodge excess amounts of enamel. If the slip seems too thick for easy draining, add water. Stir thoroughly until it is the consistency of heavy cream. After the enamel has dried it can be fired.

Preparation of the enamel. Powdered enamel, ground extremely fine—200 to 300-mesh—is made into a suitable paste by mixing it with pine or lavender oil with a touch of turpentine as thinner. With a palette knife, mix powder and oil to a tacky consistency.

Painting the tile with black enamel mixture.

The pattern can be pounced on the tile through a paper stencil.

Removing the stencil from the tile.

A hard rubber roller can be used to apply the enamel through the stencil.

70

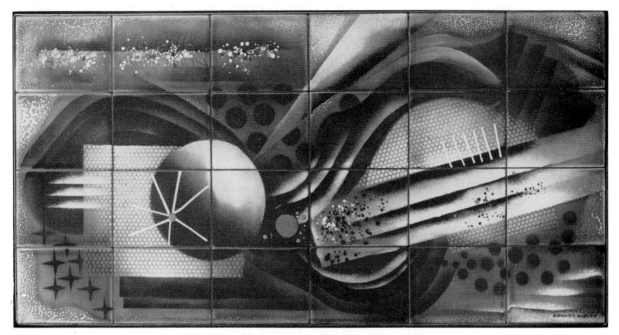

Rhythm of the Spheres. A 15 x 30-inch panel on copper comprising 24 tile sections. Note the textural variety throughout. 1938.

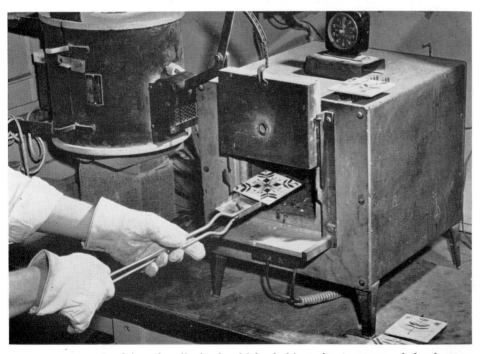

In firing the tile it should be held at the entrance of the furnace until the oils have smoked away; then it is entered into furnace for fusing.

This picture demonstrates how a mirror or decorative panel comprised of many small sections can be assembled on a piece of thin plywood. The adhesive for both mirror and sections is strong black "Miracle Adhesive," a product usually sold in hardware stores. When dome-shaped sections are used, be sure to put a generous amount of the adhesive at its corners.

Mirror made of enamel on copper sections. Each square and oblong piece was hand-shaped and domed. Sgraffito was used in the line design. Color—yellow green, black, and gold with brown leather frame. 1951.

Animal Kingdom. This 24-section mural, on 18-gauge copper, is in transparent brown and yellow enamels. The animals, fish, and birds are in opaque enamel. 1934.

Mosaics made with either transparent or opaque enamel are useful for decorating such things as serving trays, mirrors, table tops, and cigarette box inserts. They can be made in such small squares that they are within the possibilities of beginners with modest equipment.

Here is shown the assembling of small and larger squares with oblong pieces in assorted colors.

Sgraffito is a process of scratching the design through one enamel that overlays another enamel of a different color or value. In this illustration the base is a previously-fired white enamel. It has been coated with black enamel through which (before firing) the design is scratched. Excess dry powder is blown away before the piece is put into the furnace to fuse the black enamel and make the decoration permanent. A dental tool or chisel-edge hard wood stick serves for the scratching.

SGRAFFITO

Sgraffito is an Italian word meaning scratched. It is an ancient technique first used on pottery and clay wares in Bologna, Italy, before the seventeenth century. It consists of scratching away a top surface to expose a ground of another color. In the early thirties I devised a way to successfully apply this technique to enamel. With properly prepared enamels applied over a fired base coat of assorted colors, the craftsman will find this means of decorating both spontaneous and exciting.

The technique implies stylization and a modern approach to design. The better one is able to draw with spontaneity and directness, freer and

This transparent purple and blue enameled round copper plaque (18 inches) has been decorated in the sgraffito technique. Collection of John L. Hanigan, Vice President, Corning Glass Works, Corning, New York, 1955.

This transparent enamel on an 18-inch round copper plaque is a good example of sgraffito in line technique. The wide and narrow lines and the lump textures make for added interest. Collection of J. Milton Costello, Cleveland Heights, Ohio, 1951.

SECTIONAL PANEL AND BOWLS   VITREOUS ENAMEL ON COPPER   SGRAFFITO TECHNIQUE

Bowl (center) American Pavilion, Brussels World's Fair, 1958.
Bowl (lower right) Collection Dr. and Mrs. T. Keith Glennan, President of Case
Institute of Technology, Cleveland, Ohio.
Plate (lower left) enamel on aluminum.

These plaques and footed bowls are examples of sgraffito technique on vertical and flat surfaces. The spontaneous line drawing was made with a pointed tool and, after firing, the areas of the design were filled in with enamel and liquid platinum. The platinum was applied heavy in the *Water Bird* plaque and resulted in large crackle tearing of the surface. The colors are lavender, blue gray, white, black, platinum and gold. Large plaques, Collection of The Cleveland Museum of Art, 1953.

These hairlines were produced by scratching a black enamel coating of 150 to 200 mesh that was sifted onto a previously fired white base coat. A light spray of gum tragacanth was then scratched and fired at 1450°F. for two and a half minutes.

79

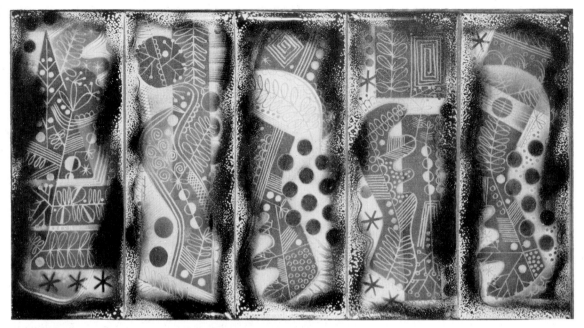

Design Rhythms. A five-sectioned 18-gauge copper panel 24 x 40 inches in the sgraffito technique. The colors are yellow, brown, black, with generous amounts of white speckled surfaces, 1953.

Other examples of line designs using color combinations of pink, white, and black. The cigarette box is black leather.

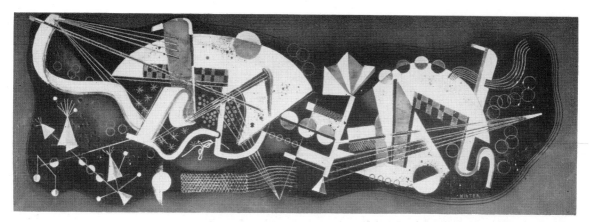

Opaque enamel on steel, 15 by 45 inches. The colors are blue, amethyst, black, white, gray, gold, and platinum. A combination of painting, drawing, and sgraffito techniques. Collection Cleveland Museum of Art, 1953.

A "Special Award" group of enameling on copper in the 1936 May Show of The Cleveland Museum of Art. The square picture, *Figure Composition,* and the *Emerald Green Punch Bowl* are in the permanent collection of The Cleveland Museum of Art.

more pleasing will be the results. With finely ground enamels one can make a line as fine as a hair or as wide as half an inch. A dental tool, a sharpened hard wood orange stick or a tooth pick will serve to produce both types and widths of linear design.

All types of subject matter are suitable for work in sgraffito. Sometimes quite realistic effects can be obtained by delicately shading a drawing in enamel (as in Limoges) after the line drawing has been made. This technique knows only the limitation of the person using it, and is an ideal way of producing designs for jewelry, brooches, cuff links, necklaces, earrings, compacts, buttons, bowls and murals.

There are several ways of working sgraffito. Usually one works on an already fired base coat of white, black, or some opaque color, sifting on it a fine, opaque cover coat through which the scratching is done. Another manner is to apply the fine enamel directly to the surface of the copper itself, and then scratch the lines of the drawing, exposing the metal. A clear flux or transparent colors can then be sifted over the top and fired. All bare surfaces of the copper must be covered when the piece is entered into the furnace; otherwise the heat will oxidize the bare metal.

Woodlands. 25 by 30 inches. A white sgraffito line drawing makes this an effective decoration. Brown, turquoise, chartreuse, with red and black accents. Collection of Albert Mayer, Architect, New York City, 1949.

82

If a white line pattern is desired, apply a coat of hard, white, opaque enamel, 80-mesh, to copper and fire in the customary manner. Using a large camel's-hair brush, coat the entire surface with a thin solution of gum tragacanth and water. Keep the surface free from finger marks so that the gum coating doesn't separate. Almost immediately sift on a black 200-mesh powder enamel using a 150 or 200-mesh sieve. This should not be too thick but just enough to cover the white surface completely. A light spray gum solution with a fixatif mouth blower should then be used to dampen the surface, but not too much to cause the enamel to run.

After the piece has dried out, the design can be scratched into the black enamel exposing the white base under it. It can then be fired for about two minutes at 1500° F. Other colors, gold or lusters, can then be applied if desired and fired again. Interesting effects can be obtained by using soft enamels over hard ones, or hard enamels over soft, opaque enamels over soft fluxes. Sometimes overfiring will produce a separation of the colors and interesting crackles or speckles will develop. Overglazed colors also have unlimited possibilities for sgraffito technique. After applying them they must be dried for best results.

Abstraction. Transparent brown enamel on copper panel 20 by 40 inches. Black underlying pattern, with white speckled edge adding to quality of the work. Collection Syracuse Museum of Fine Arts, Syracuse, N. Y., 1952.

A 22-inch shallow bowl with pronounced crackle effect. An extended firing time will melt the enamel to a greater degree and produce wider lines.

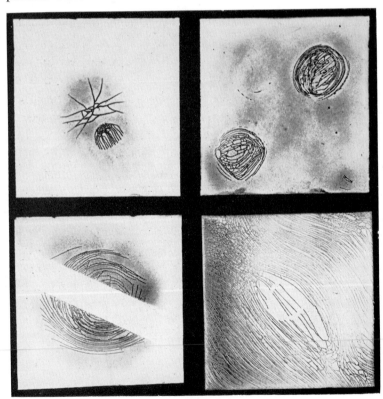

Examples of controlled crackle. The crazing lines appear only where a soft flux enamel has been applied as an undercoating.

CRAZING, CRACKLE, AND EGG SHELL

Crazing, crackle or tearing of enamel surfaces during firing is produced by the reaction of one type of enamel on another. When a hard enamel is applied over a soft one, the crazing develops as the softer surface melts and pulls the harder top surface which hasn't begun to melt. On convex or concave surfaces the tearing is usually greater, due to the flowing of the enamel. In one of my early experiments, I discovered that opaque enamel, ground in a ball mill, with clear clay as a setting-up agent, produced a creamy liquid slip after three-and-a-half or four hours' grinding. Liquid slips can be produced in assorted colors by the addition, in the mill, of metallic oxides. When such an enamel is applied over a previously fired, transparent flux or transparent color, the result is a tearing, crackle effect. According to the temperature and the length of firing time, thin or wide tearings will be produced. This was one of of my personal developments in 1934.

This technique can be beautiful if treated with restraint, but if garish colors are used, the results will be crude and harsh. These liquid enamels can be purchased from suppliers.

It is possible to "spot control" the area of crackle by applying the soft flux only in certain areas where the crackle is desired. One can produce a very fine hairline tearing by the thinness of the undercoating, the thinness of the slip coat, and the appropriate firing time. Black-and-white combinations are good, as are brown and white, turquoise and brown, pink and white, lavender and light blue, and gray and white. Gold, silver, platinum and assorted lusters can be used to produce metallic crackling on fired enamel surfaces. Crackles properly used can produce "one of a kind" effects.

Egg-shell sheeting has been one of my most recent developments (made by applying and firing opaque enamel on a sheet of mica, and lifting off when cool). This thin sheet of fired opaque enamel can then be picked up with the fingers and broken with a sharp tool over a fired black surface. The surface must first be coated with gum tragacanth, slightly thicker than is customary, and the white sheeting placed over it with a light pressing of the fingers and pointed tool. Cracks will then appear in the enamel. These can be opened as wide as desired by the fingers. After drying, the piece can be fired for about two minutes at 1450° F.

Crackle—Egg shell. A piece of very thin white enamel sheeting is ready to be laid upon a gummed tragacanth surface of gloss black enamel. The thin enamel, being very fragile, must be handled carefully. The sheeting is made by applying a thin coating of opaque white enamel on a piece of mica and firing it. The enamel sheet is removed when the mica cools. Although very thin, the sheeting can be held carefully without breaking.

Here the sheeting, punched with a sharp tool, breaks up. The fragments can be opened to any width by pushing them apart with the fingers. Upon drying, the piece can be fired for two minutes at 1450° F.

Night and Day. An example of the use of crackle and sgraffito
in a transparent and opaque enameled copper panel 24 x 36 inches.
Black, white, and turquoise with generous amounts of clear flux.

Silver foil is used on this serving tray, box, and ash tray. Transparent turquoise is applied and fired over the foil. Dark blue, black, and white speckles are other colors used. Serving tray in the collection of Mr. and Mrs. Harry B. Field, Shaker Heights, Ohio, 1931.

SILVER AND GOLD FOIL AND PAILLONS

Silver and gold foil can be purchased from the manufacturer in the form of small paper-thin sheets; the gold leaf is the same foil as used by sign painters, silver foil is heavier. Silver foil was used by the traditional artists to produce a more luminous surface than regular transparent enamels on copper or silver. Foil is always used over a previously fired enamel surface, and when transparent colors are lightly sifted over the foil and fired the result is one of the most exciting and luminous forms of the enameler's art.

Gold foil is thinner and more difficult to use than silver foil. Single sheets have a tendency to burn up in the intense heat; however, the use of four or five sheets together will produce good results. Use xx-23 K Hastings Patent gold leaf and apply a very thin gum solution between four or five sheets. Place thin protective paper on top and bottom of the pack and draw your design on the top sheet, then cut through all sheets with a sharp razor blade or X-acto knife.

Next pounce the pack with a very sharp needle, producing several air holes for moisture to escape; then remove paper from the bottom and top of the pile. Apply a thin solution of gum and water to the enamel surface and place the cutout gold leaf design on it. After drying thoroughly, burnish with a wad of cotton, then fire. If desired, for better wearing quality and a transparent hard protection, hard clear flux can be fused over the gold.

Paillon is the name given to tiny die-stamped ornaments or motifs made from sheets of silver, gold or platinum foil and applied over opaque or transparent enamel surfaces. The technique originated in Germany and Austria. During the early turn of the twentieth century, many commercial enameled articles were turned out using paillons and transparent enamels. Some of the designs include dots, stars, leaves, crosses, flowers, birds, fish, fruit and many other interesting motifs. On firing, the paillons sink slightly into the enamel surface. To preserve them, a light coating of transparent flux or transparent colored enamel is applied and fired over them. It is possible to make some simple paillon shapes by using sheet silver or gold leaf and cutting small dots or stars out with a sharp knife or scissors. Place the foil between two sheets of paper for easier cutting.

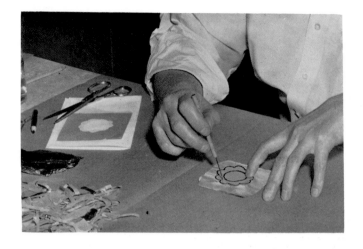

A sheet of silver foil is placed between two pieces of paper. A needle point punching through the design on the top paper makes tiny holes through the foil which will allow moisture or air to escape when being fired.

Holding the foil and papers tightly so they will not slip, cut out the design with scissors.

Wet the surface of the ash tray with thin gum tragacanth solution. Press the piece of foil onto the surface so that there are no wrinkled or uneven areas. After drying the piece can be fired in the furnace at 1450°F. for about two minutes. Remove from furnace and stroke lightly with a glass brush (purchased from any supplier) before the piece has had a chance to cool, to smooth out any irregularities or wrinkles in the foil.

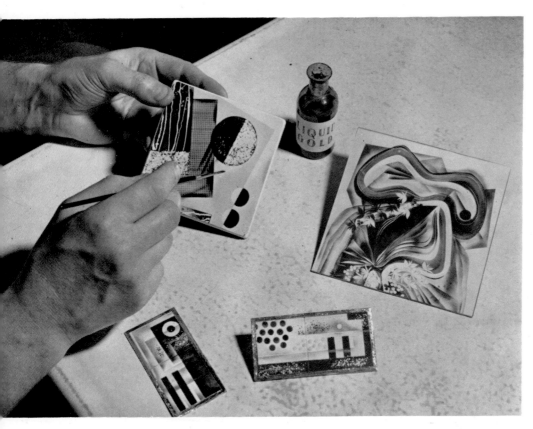

Liquid gold is applied to a square enamel tile with a pointed camel's-hair brush. The application of gold and other precious metals always comes in the last firing. Furnace temperature should be approximately 1350°F. with a two to three minute timing period.

LIQUID GOLD, SILVER, PLATINUM, AND LUSTERS

Liquid bright gold is an alloy of gold, rhodium, fluxes, and other base metal compounds that are dissolved in solvents and volatile oils. The gold is susceptible to volatilization when fired, due to its thin application of about four millionths of an inch; therefore, rhodium, which has a much higher boiling point than gold, is added to the liquid bright gold to act as a protector for the gold. The flux acts to fuse the gold to the surface of the opaque or transparent enamel.

Liquid gold comes in various viscosities for different uses and methods of applications, such as lining, banding, hand-design work, and spraying. The oils and solvents are so compounded as to let the gold decoration dry in air of normal room temperature in less than one hour. If necessary, this drying time can be shortened by mechanical drying in an oven or over a heating plate. The quicker the drying, the less opportunity there is for the gold to pick up lint, dust or moisture. Lint or large dust particles fired in gold will fire out as black spots, and any moisture will fire out as white spots.

Liquid gold is almost always used as an overglaze type of decoration, but it can be used also as an underglaze coating with a thin coat of transparent enamel fused directly over it. Camel's-hair or red sable brushes are usually used in applying the gold; fine tip brushes for fine lines and heavier brushes for covering large surfaces.

To cover a relatively smooth surface, the piece can be held at a slight angle and the gold stroked across the surface much as one would handle a watercolor wash. Each successive stroke joins the previous one, and the work should be done quickly for good results. Once the

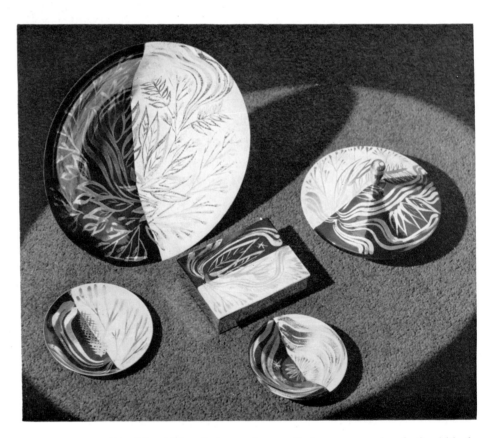

Liquid gold brush decoration applied over a previously fired black-and-white surface. The bowl, covered dish, cigarette box, and ash tray make a related group.

Decorative accessories in transparent and opaque enamel on copper. Colors are brown, white, chartreuse, and gold.

gold is applied, don't go back over it. If the liquid gold becomes too thick to flow freely, either in a brush or mechanical airbrush, it may be thinned with gold essence. This should be used sparingly, as too much will weaken the color of the gold. If used too thin, it may result in a pinkish film after firing. If applied too heavily, it may either burn away completely or tear and cause scumming and blistering. If, in firing, the gold surface burns away, another coat may be applied and the work refired.

Great care must be taken when decorating with liquid gold as finger marks will leave a purplish smudge when fired, even though it appears the smear was completely wiped off the pieces. In firing, the oils must be smoked off first. This can be done by holding the work at the open door of the furnace, putting it in and out for a minute or two. When the smoking has stopped, the piece can be placed in the furnace for two or three minutes at approximately 1350° F. If not bright and completely fused, it can be left a longer time at 1450° F. to 1500° F.

Brushes can be cleaned in nitrobenzene and carbon tetrachloride. Two bottles can be used; the first for rinsing, and the other to clean them thoroughly. As a final washing, warm water and soap will leave the brush soft and ready for use another time.

The same general procedure is to be followed when firing *liquid silver* and *platinum*. Only through personal experience will one learn the fascinating effects possible with liquid precious metals.

Metallic lusters were first employed on clay wares. The origin is quite uncertain, but it is believed to have been initiated by the Arabs around about the ninth century. The Persians are probably best known for their excellent lusterware in ceramics. Its real origin was probably due to the primitive methods of firing and the concentrated reducing conditions produced by those methods. In such work, evidence of luster tendencies would inevitably be revealed, its beauty making a strong appeal to the creative instincts of the craftsman. The same luster possibilities await the present-day enameler that were experienced by the ancient Persian and Moorish potters.

It might be well to remember that the softer enamels produce better luster surfaces than the extremely hard ones. In the production of silver luster, the salts consist of silver sulphide, silver carbonate, silver cyanide, and silver nitrate. Copper oxide, copper carbonate, and copper sulphate, are used for ruby lusters. In all experiments with fusing and getting good results with lusters, it is advisable to make careful notes of application, firing temperature, and of every detail of procedure. The room where lusters are being applied should be free from dust and excessive humidity.

Bowls, trays, covered dish, and cigarette box in transparent brown with liquid gold leaf design. The white speckled edge adds texture and quality to the work. The box is brown leather.

AUTHOR FIRING PANELS IN LABORATORY FURNACE

Small and useful accessories in opaque and transparent enamels on copper. The powder bowl at the left is a hand hammered piece in transparent lemon-yellow enamel, with polished brass balls on the top. Other objects are in black, white, brown, and green with a generous use of liquid gold.

STEPS IN MAKING A CLOISONNÉ ENAMEL VASE

Assorted lumps of opaque colored frit in foreground are ground to an 80-mesh powder and then used to fill in the cloisson areas.

1. Smooth plain copper vase cleaned and ready for coating of clear flux to be applied and fired.

2. The small flat wires are bent into their desired shapes and stuck to the sides of the vase with heavy gum tragacanth. In the firing process the wires sink into the flux enamel and, when cooled, are permanently adhered to the piece.

3. First application of background colors and foreground blossom colors.

4. Enamel in fusing has a tendency to shrink, so possibly two applications will be necessary, with each one being fired before cloissons are filled to the desired level.

5. So as to produce an even surface the enamel is used slightly above the top edges of the wires and the entire surface ground down with a rubbing stone so that the enamel and the top edges of the wires are at the same level.

6. After the grinding operation, the vase must again be put into the furnace to bring back the gloss to the enamel. A final buffing on a felt or cotton wheel with rouge will produce a high polish on the exposed edges of the wires.

Twentieth Century Chinese cloisonné in the Metropolitan Museum of Art.

CLOISONNÉ

Cloisonné is of great antiquity and is essentially Asiatic. It is a process which requires great manual dexterity and no less patience. The technique consists of decorating any metal article of plain or shaped surface by means of flat thin wires which are bent to the outline of the design, thus forming cells called "cloisons." These cells are filled with different colored enamels and then fired.

The wires are usually made of brass, copper, gold, silver or steel. For small work, these flat wires may be purchased in widths of 1/32, 1/16, and 1/8 of an inch. Cloisonné panels and murals may be produced with wires 1/8 or 1/4-inch wide. All wires, no matter what width or thickness, must first be annealed with a torch or in the furnace until the metal turns red. They can be cooled and pickled in sulphuric acid and water in the usual percentage mixture.

When the design has been decided upon, a working drawing and the article to be decorated are prepared. The first step is faithfully to reproduce the design in the flat metal wire. As this is no easy task, a simple design is advised for one's first experiments. Avoid complicated, broken lines, except in the case of shaped articles, where the contours will necessitate the use of short wires. Long straight wires and disconnected pieces must also be avoided, as these would probably fall

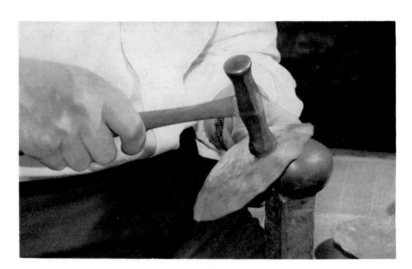

First step in making a cloisonné enamel; the copper disk is shaped over a dome stake.

A ring foot is soldered onto the bottom with hard silver solder. Borax is a suitable flux to use in fusing the solder. The piece is wired onto a chrome wire screen and placed upon a tripod.

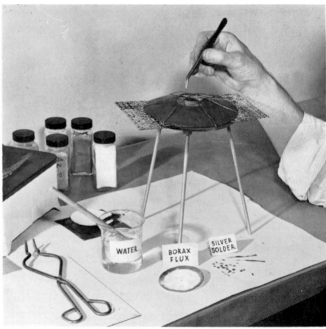

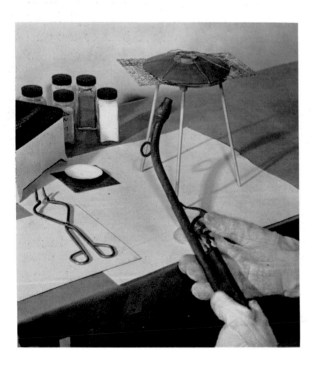

The soldering is done by applying intense heat with a torch or by placing the work in the furnace until the solder has melted.

A fine, flat-edged wire in brass, copper, silver or steel will serve to make the cloisons. The design should, of course, first be drawn on paper; then the wire cut to lengths required to follow the pattern. After each small piece of wire is cut it should be annealed with hand torch to remove its temper and prevent loss of its shape when the piece goes into the furnace.

After the copper plate has been pickled and cleaned, a soft clear flux is sifted on and the piece fired. After the small wire has been annealed and bent into the desired shape it can be dipped into a rather thick gum tragacanth solution with tweezers and set in position on the piece. The gum will hold it in place until the entire piece is completed and put in the furnace. In the 1500°F. temperature for one minute the wires become permanently affixed to the metal.

With the use of a flat-edged tool the ground enamel, in dampened form, can be picked up and placed in the desired areas of the cloissons.

over on their sides during the firing instead of remaining verticle. These are important points not to be overlooked when the designs are being prepared.

To reproduce the outlines of the design correctly, a few special tools will be required: tweezers, mandrel, and a pair of small metal shears. Many traditional enamelers soldered the wire cloisons to the base metal and then filled in the areas with colored enamels. A more modern method is to coat the metal with a flux or rather soft opaque or transparent enamel and by dipping the small wires into gum tragacanth solution and applying the wet wires to the fired surface of the enamel, the wires sink into the enamel when the piece is again fired lightly. The cloisons can then be filled with suitable colored enamels and fired again.

During the first firing the enamel shrinks and sinks below the level of the cloisons which have to be refilled and fired again. Three or four firings may thus be needed to completely fill the cells.

After the last coat application and firing, the piece must be "stoned" with a carborundum rubbing stone or emery stick. This will expose the upper edges of the wires and leave both them and the enamel on the same surface. After a vigorous brushing with pumice powder and water to remove all traces of the emery, the piece must be washed off with clear water and dried. The final operation is to fire it once more to bring out the gloss in the enamel, and to brighten the top edges of the wires a buffing with a felt wheel and rouge compound is necessary.

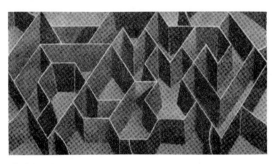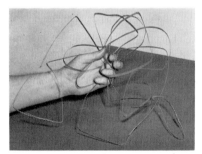

Cold-rolled enameling steel band about ¼-inch wide (right) is available for larger scale architectural cloisonné work. The band wire should be annealed with torch to remove its temper so it can be worked easily. The wire must be brazed onto a metal sheeting, then the piece is cleaned and pickled ready to receive the enamel. Assorted large lumps of colored frit can be used to fill in the areas of the pattern. Steel bands of 22-gauge thickness and ½-inch width (left) are also available for architectural cloisonné. With these wide bands the craftsman can dispense with the steel backing, and through the use of transparent enamels achieve a plique-à-jour or stained glass effect when light is placed behind it.

CHAMPLEVÉ

This traditional technique consists of hollowing the design out of the metal surface to be decorated with an engraving tool, eating it away with a concentrated acid solution, or by mechanically stamping it with dies. The champs or cells thus produced are filled with enamel to the level of the top surface of the metal.

Of the three methods die stamping is easiest and most generally used, but for work that is rather complicated in design, the deep etch with sulphuric or nitric acid and water solution can be used effectively. *Acids must always be poured into the water* and heavy rubber gloves should be worn to insure safety. The areas of the metal that are not to be etched must be protected from the acid by painting them with asphaltum, thinned slightly so it can readily be brushed on. The parts of the design that are to be depressed in the metal will be left bare for this action of the acid. Regular wax coatings used in etchings can also serve as a resist.

The design on paper can be transferred onto the metal with a piece of carbon paper. A deep Pyrex bowl or stone crock can be used for the pickling solution, and the metal can be left in the acid solution until it has been eaten away to the desired depth.

Turpentine will remove the asphaltum. The piece should be rinsed in clear water and all edges should be brushed with a wire brush to insure the removal of all acid.

After the piece has dried, the first coat of enamel can be applied in the cells. It usually takes two or three applications of enamel and subsequent firings before the enamel reaches the level of the metal. The last coat should fire slightly over the surface of the metal, as it can be ground or stoned down with rubbing stone and pumice powder and water. A last firing will return the gloss to the enamel. The bare metal is then highly polished in the usual way.

Early Thirteenth Century French champlevé enamel chest in The Cleveland Museum of Art.

After the piece has been enameled and fired (champlevé process) it can be polished lightly with very fine steel wool. A very weak solution of sulphuric acid and water will aid in removing any stubborn copper oxidation. Caution must be taken not to etch the gloss off the enameled surface. Buffing with felt buffer and rouge will give the metal a high polish. Opaque white enamel covers the depressed pattern areas of this bowl; the darker areas are polished copper.

104

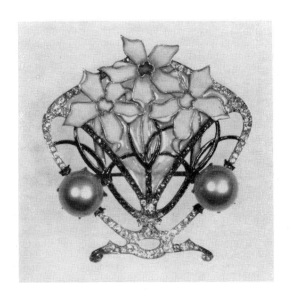

Plique-à-jour jewelry by René Jules Lalique of France, about 1900. Transparent enamel on gold with pearl settings. The piece is 2¼ x 2¼ inches.

PLIQUE-À-JOUR

This style of enameling has a similarity to cloisonné. This technique may be used for such articles as cups, saucers, plates, vases, spoon handles, small panels, and jewelry. These articles show their true value and quality when placed where a bright light can pass through them in the manner of a stained-glass window.

It is necessary to use translucent or transparent enamels in filling the cloisons, in a manner similar to the cloisonné process, but it differs slightly in that thin copper is used for the base which is kept free from any enamel application on its reverse side. After the cloisons have been filled with the desired enamel colors and fired, the enamel surface is painted with asphaltum or wax and the piece immersed in a strong solution of nitric acid. After a few minutes in the acid bath the bare copper back side will have been eaten away except for a small retaining band of metal around the edge of the piece that has been covered with an asphaltum coating for protection. Upon cleaning off the asphaltum or wax, a true plique-à-jour will appear. There are many ways of producing fine work with this technique, such as working on sheets of mica, removing the mica after the enamel has dried and has been fired. The use of perforated metals and wire screening also make it possible to acquire similar results by fusing transparent enamel over the metal and having the light pass through the openings which hold the enamel.

Plique-à-jour effect can be produced with perforated metals. The metal should be cleaned and thoroughly dried. Using an 80-mesh powdered enamel over a previously painted design, the holes in the metal will hold the clear enamel by capillary attraction. Several coats may be needed to cover completely. The effect will simulate a stained-glass window. Note the reflection of the hand through the mesh openings.

Footed bowls — transparent enamel on silver — are ten and twelve inches in diameter. The reverse sides of these bowls are left bare polished metal; however, because of silver tarnishing, it is best to enamel the backs of all pieces.

PLAQUE, PLATES, AND FOOTED BOWLS

Plate (*right*), enamel on aluminum; footed bowl (*right*), transparent lime enamel on silver;
peacock plaque (*center*), enamel on stainless steel; square plate (*Collection Harry T.
Marks*, Cleveland, Ohio); footed bowl (*front*), and powder box, transparent enamel on copper.

ENAMELING SILVER AND STEEL

Pure or fine silver (0.295) can be enameled successfully with transparent or opaque enamels. But it seems a shame to cover a beautiful silver surface with opaque enamel, so I recommend using only transparent or translucent enamels which will let the brilliance of the metal shine through. Enamels made for silver are of slightly different composition from copper enamels, but the process of firing and application is quite similar. Silver is considerably more expensive than sheet copper or steel, and for this reason it is not used as extensively.

Sheet silver is harder and more rigid than copper and, when a bowl comes from the heat of the furnace, quick handling is necessary to true all edges before the metal cools and enamel hardens. Colors enameled on silver are higher in key than those applied on copper, due to its purity and whiteness. The colors that look best on silver are pearl gray, turquoise, opals, pinks, sky blue, yellow, and chartreuse. Oftentimes a hard clear flux is used over the silver and a transparent color fired over it.

Good grades of silver-plated sheet steel can be purchased from the metal supplied. A fine grade of steel called "enameling stock" can be enameled with opaque enamels. A bluish ground coat, however, is necessary for a first coat and, after firing, white or colors may be applied over the top and again fired. Silver-plated steel can also be enameled successfully.

Fine silver makes an ideal base for transparent enamels. The metal, while not as soft as copper, can be easily shaped, drawn, and planished. On the oblong dish, the hand planishing marks can be seen easily through the light transparent yellow enamel. Black threads and gold were used for decoration. The round bowls are light blue and pale green. Transparent enamels on silver have a higher tonal value than enamels on copper due to the brilliance of the metal.

A buffet service in colorful enameled aluminum. Sgraffito technique
was used on the serving tray and canapé plate. The insides of the
tall cups were not enameled but highly polished.

ENAMELING ALUMINUM

Considerable research has been going on for the past eight or ten years to develop and perfect a low-temperature vitreous enamel for aluminum. The E. I. Du Pont de Nemours Company has perfected aluminum frits and these enamels are now on the commercial market. This development has satisfied a long felt need for an impervious protective color coating for aluminum, and permits the full utilization of aluminum's desirable lightweight properties.

The Ferro Corporation has also been doing research on leadless enamels for aluminum, and it considers that the future holds great promise for this material. Aluminum enamels have excellent resistance to impact, flexibility and thermal shock. They are not affected by acids, alkalies or sulphides.

Enameled aluminum may be sheared, cut and drilled with very little, if any, marring of the enamel surface. Also, limited forming can be done after firing. A very wide color range is possible by using metallic oxides. Many surface variations are possible and most any degree of reflectivity from dull mat to extremely high gloss can be achieved. Panels heated to 1000°F. have been plunged into cold water with no crackling or flaking of the enamel.

Aluminum of any thickness, ranging from thin foil to heavy castings and assorted gauges in sheets, can be enameled successfully. Welding can also be done on the reverse side without discoloration or damage to the enamel surface. Enamel can even be applied over welds.

Enamels may be applied on wrought 61S, 2S, and 3S aluminum alloys and on nonporous castings of #43 alloy. For extrusions, 53S, 62S, and 63S can be used. The degree of temper in the metal appears to be no factor in its enameling properties, although softer tempers are more generally suitable for forming operations.

There is, however, some distortion in thin, nonrigid sections which are enameled on only one side; but these sections can be straightened by cold rolling without damaging the surface. Distortion is negligible when sections are enameled on both sides. Corners and edges should be rounded to a radius of not less than 1/32 inch.

With cast alloys, it is essential that the metal be substantially free from porosity and sand holes to prevent tearing of the enamel. Quality control in the foundry is necessary to prevent such defects. It is important to have a clean, active surface, free from grease and oil.

The metal may be given a pretreating by a fifteen minute immersion in the following acid bath at room temperature: 0.25% "Duponol," WA flakes fatty alcohol sodium sulfate or 6.0% sulphuric acid and 93.75% water or a strong detergent such as "Dreft." Articles that have been fabricated with wax or tallow-type lubricants should be degreased in solvent solution before immersion in the acid cleaner. A wooden tank or steel tank lined with rubber or lead may be used for the acid bath. After cleaning, the metal should be thoroughly rinsed and drained.

For the worker or craftsmen with small aluminum objects, the cleaning and pickling operation can be a more simple one. Small pieces of aluminum have been successfully enameled by just preheating the metal for six minutes in the furnace at 1000°F., due regard being given to their high alkalinity and lead content which is present in a high percentage of the frits. One should be careful to avoid dust inhalation; workers should wash thoroughly before eating and permit no food to be brought into the working area. Enamels should not be used on aluminum surfaces that come in contact with food or liquids. Newly developed leadless enamels can now be used for surfaces that will come in contact with foods and liquids.

To cover large surfaces, enamels can be ground fine and sprayed onto the metal and, for the small user, the frit can be finely ground and sifted on, similar to copper enamels. One must wear a respirator over the nose and mouth if any dusting or sieving is done.

There are several different types of aluminum enamels, a ground coat as well as cover coats. Certain frits are made primarily for whites and pastels while cadmium-containing enamels are recommended for reds, yellows, oranges, and pinks. Unlike the general use of copper enamels which are ground to 80-mesh, all aluminum enamels are ground to from 250 to 300-mesh. For dry process application the grind could be about 200-mesh.

Since aluminum itself melts at approximately 1200°F., a very accurate temperature control must be followed in firing. This should not exceed 1000°F. for a period of from six to seven minutes for any piece of metal, regardless of size. Flat sheets of thin enameled aluminum can be adhered to plywood or honeycombed paper backing by adhesive, heat, and pressure.

The panel in the background is a 30 x 45-inch sheet aluminum of .025 thickness. Colors are blue, red, white, and gold. The two bowls at left are in the permanent collection of the Ceramic Research Institute, Calcutta, India. 1957.

The possibilities for artistic expression with aluminum enamels are as great as those of copper or steel enamels. The assorted transparent color frits comparable to copper frits are still not available, but will undoubtedly be placed on the market when the demand arises for them. One of the advantages with aluminum is that any given area of a design pattern can be left bare metal and receive a high polish to give the effect of fine silver. The insides of bowls can be enameled and the outside left bare metal and then polished to a high satin luster. This metal offers an exciting challenge to the creative artist and designer.

Architectural panels as well as abstract third-dimensional sculpture should find ready use and acceptance. Where light weight is a requisite, marine construction, lounge and staterooms, trains and planes should readily accept this colorful permanent material. The industrial field can utilize it in stoves, refrigerators, furniture, table tops, elevator doors, cabs, and store fronts. Aluminum enamels may also be used on aluminized steel.

A 16-inch enameled aluminum bowl in sgraffito technique. Collection Aluminum Development Association of Great Britain, London. 1954.

Drawing technique. Drawing with a white enamel pencil, especially designed for this purpose and available at supply houses, is most suitable for large surfaces. It affords the artist much freedom of expression. The pattern area may be filled-in with colored enamels or with golds or lusters. The white lines remain after the piece has been fired but will fade upon repeated firings or if the furnace is too hot.

DRAWING AND INLAY ON ENAMEL

A specially compounded drawing pencil is now available through one of my discoveries and will soon be marketed for general use. Holding it in the hand, like any pencil, one can draw white lines on black or dark colored enamel surfaces which can be fused at approximately 1450°F. for about two minutes. The white lines will not fire away in the process; however, one must be careful not to get finger marks or grease on the enamel that is to receive the drawing. Enamel colors, liquid gold, or lusters can then be painted in the desired parts of the design and again fired in the usual way.

To further complete a design, straight edges of paper acting as a stencil can be used to cover the edge of the area that will not receive the powdered enamel. This simplified manner of working is much easier and quicker than the technique of inlaying wet enamel with a spatula. Dark lines can be made on a white opaque enamel surface by using a piece of ordinary lead, like that of a fishline sinker.

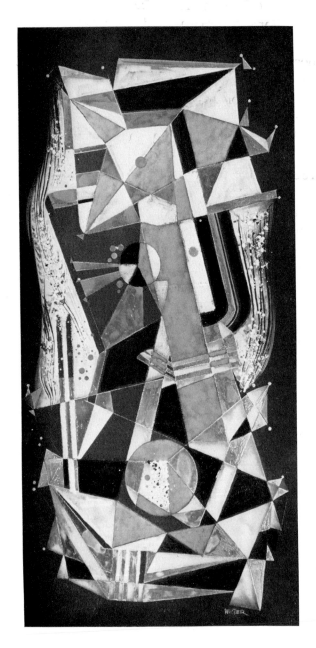

Mexican Fiesta. An 18 x 40-inch panel in drawing and inlay techniques. The design was first penciled-in with white enamel pencil on a glossy black, fired, opaque enamel. Then the colors were applied to different areas. A few lumps of frit contribute textural interest.

Decorative enamel bowls, boxes, candlesticks, vases, ash trays, murals, cabinet door knobs, and many other objects have for many years been colorful accessories in the home interior. They give quality and warmth to fabrics, woods, metals, leathers, and other materials when placed on or near them or incorporated with them. Many of these can be made with the use of only a small furnace.

Small mosaic sections of copper can be cut and enameled to make colorful inlays in cabinet doors, table tops, trays, and even fireplaces. Larger furnaces make it possible to produce large, textural designs for wall partitions, murals, fireplace fronts, lamp bases, and floor screens. Enameled tiles have unlimited possibilities in the decoration of bathrooms and kitchens.

Enamel treated in a dull mat finish on heavy gauge steel or cast iron makes ideal flooring for porch or patio. Rough textures in mat enamels produce a slip-proof surface for this purpose.

It is the home that is most likely to invite the creative interests of the craftsman because we naturally strive to make our homes as beautiful as possible. Enamels not only provide great beauty in design and color; they are very practical since they are easy to clean and are, of course, fireproof.

A list of objects which can be made for the home:

After-dinner coffee cups	Finger bowls
Album inserts and covers	Fireplace fronts
Ash trays	Floor screens
Bar tops	Flower bowls
Bathroom walls and floors	Fountains
Book ends	Lamps
Book inserts	Mirror frames
Bottle-opener handles	Name plates
Candelabras	Napkin rings
Candy boxes	Paperweights
Cigarette cups	Picture frames
Clock dials	Place mats
Clocks (table and wall)	Powder boxes
Coasters	Silent butlers
Coffee-table tops	Table lighter
Compacts and lipstick holders	Trays
Door knobs	Trivets
Drawer knobs and handles	Vases

Decorative accessories in black and white opaque enamels with gold leaf decoration on copper for use in the home. The lamp, boxes, and the trays are finished in smooth, grained, black leather. The enamel lamp insert is in sgraffito which allows the luminous surface of the copper to shine through.

Fireplace mural on a steel panel with string textures. Jane L. Hansen Interiors, Cleveland, Ohio.

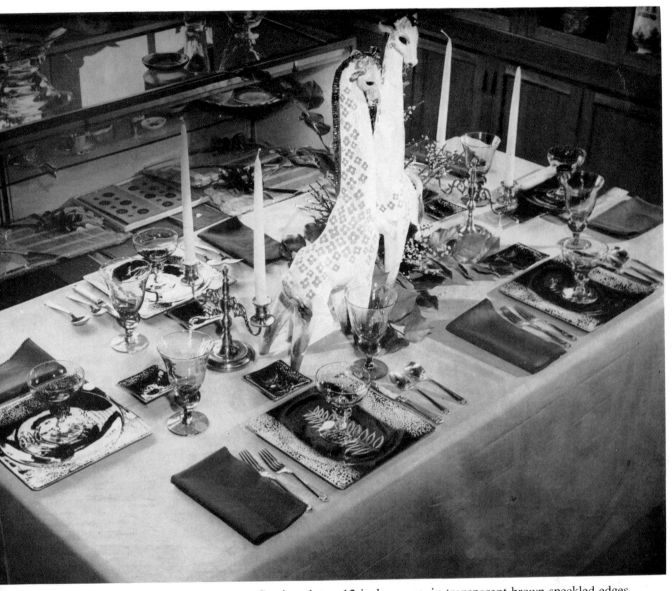

Service plates, 12-inch square, in transparent brown speckled edges and gold leaf center with matching square hand-hammered ash trays, harmonize with beige table cloth and dark brown linen napkins. The giraffe ceramic sculpture center piece was executed by Thelma Frazier Winter.

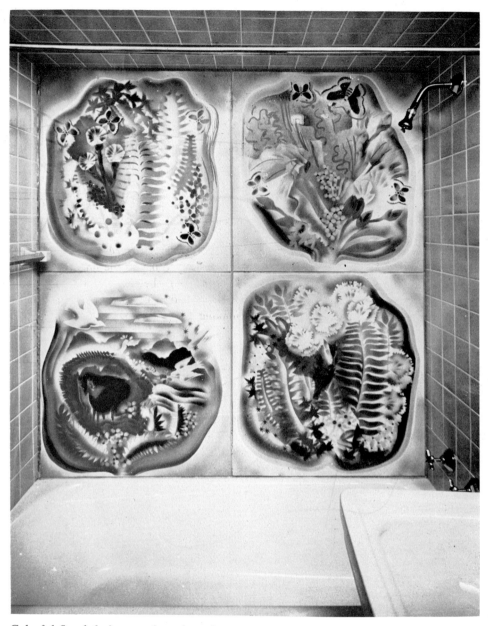

Colorful floral designs on four three-foot square panels of 16-gauge steel make an effective bathroom mural. Residence of Dr. and Mrs. G. H. McIntyre. Cleveland Heights, Ohio, 1941.

Amusing animals can be cut out of 22 or 24-gauge sheet copper, and bent and twisted into desired forms by the fingers and pointed pliers. After cleaning and pickling the pieces they can be dried and dipped into white or colored opaque enamel slip (as shown in the demonstration of making an enamel tile). After dipping, all excess enamel must be shaken off and the piece dried and fired in the usual way.

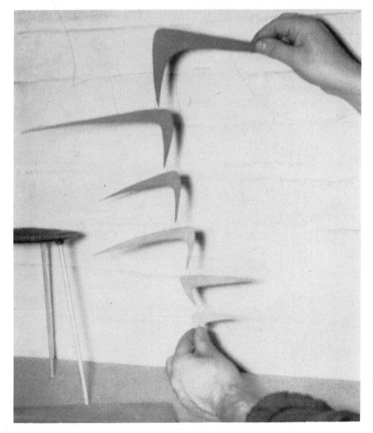

Mobiles and free-form shapes enameled in bright opaque and transparent colors. Small holes can be drilled into the edges for easy assembly with wire rings.

Greeting cards in enameled metal. Both sides of these pieces on 20-gauge copper are enameled in white slip, dried and fired. Needle point firing pins can be used for supports during firing; or the pieces can be fired while resting on its edge on a specially devised chromel support. Green or brown felt can be cemented on the back side to cover firing pin marks. All enameling techniques can be used for designs and lettering.

Steel or copper door knobs decorated with enameled designs and fired for a permanent finish.

Enameled steel sectional murals by the author produce a colorful and permanent decorative front to Herman Pitchner Theater restaurant, Cleveland, Ohio. The door frame, marquee and framework around the murals are stainless steel. J. Milton Dyer, Architect.

ENAMEL IN ARCHITECTURE

Vitreous enamel has had an important function in architecture for many years. Today it is recognized as an ideal surfacing material for all types of interior and exterior walls. It has often been wrongly promoted as a substitute for older and more familiar materials such as brick, stone or wood, but it should be recognized and used for the sake of its own peculiar characteristics which give it a unique place in the decoration and building arts.

This unique material, glass fused on metal, has all the virtues of fine china combined with the structural strength of steel. There are no set limits to the choice of color, design, or surface texture. Once fused, its surface appearance is fixed for an unlimited life span. Technical research has added acid resistance to a durable, weatherproof and fireproof material. This makes enamel impervious to all ordinary acids encountered in city air or in the average chemical laboratory. There are now ways to bond a layer of insulating material to the inside face of enameled surfaces. The sun's heat, the winter's cold, and the noise of city streets cannot penetrate the space it protects.

Detail of one of the restaurant panels.

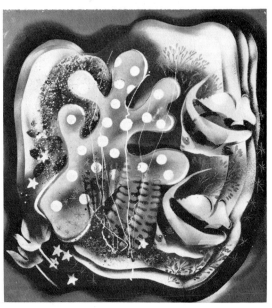

Angel Fish. Opaque and transparent enamel. A 36-inch square steel panel showing the use of lump and string textures with liquid gold. Collection The Metropolitan Museum of Art. New York, 1948.

124

Four enameled steel panels by the author in Dor-
sel's Open Grill Restaurant in Cleveland, Ohio.

Enamel on steel, copper or aluminum makes a practical and colorful surface for elevator doors.

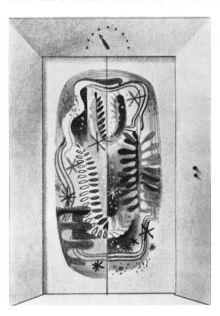

Modern construction demands prefabricated parts for speed and flexibility. Vitreous enamel sheets or panels can be obtained today in any size one desires. The sheet can be flanged, curved or flat, and in almost any shape. This gives the architect and designer almost unlimited freedom in his decorative planning. Enamel-steel, copper and aluminum panels are very easily put together. The first operation is to fix metal supporting clips to the framework of the building. The panels are attached to this framework and conceal the clips. The joints are then caulked and the job is done.

Demolition and salvage is as easy and practical as the original operation. Enameled wall areas are as easy to wash clean as are china dishes. The light weight of enameled steel and the extreme light weight of enameled aluminum make these materials especially practical as "skin" for large office and industrial buildings. There is no longer any reason why tons of limestone and brick should be raised hundreds of feet in the air to provide a surface for buildings. All contemporary architects appreciate and accept enamel panels as perfect exterior and interior curtain wall veneers for modern structures.

The prime need for commercial structures today is long life, combined with flexibility and low cost. Enamel offers all these qualities and in addition provides an unlimited variety of surface colors, designs, and unusual textures. It is ideal for lobby walls, passages, elevator cabs and doors, partitions, murals, flooring, fireplaces, and many other surfaces. Architects, artists, and designers with imagination can do much toward popularizing the material and increasing the demand for its use.

The permanence of enamel in itself is a factor of greatest importance. To have pioneered enamel mural art, in 1934, was one of my greatest thrills. Many unique enamel murals and restaurant building fronts that I have executed during the past few years show no fading of color or loss of surface qualities whatsoever.

ENAMELS FOR CHURCHES

Enamel has a long history of service in ecclesiastical arts. Byzantine artists, from the ninth century on, used enamels in their icons. They were particularly attracted by its intrinsic beauty and translucent, jewellike quality, synchronized with the use of inlays of gold and precious stones. One of the techniques they employed was plique-à-jour (explained on page 114). Other early icons were of the cloisonné type dated to the eleventh and twelfth centuries using pure gold as a base metal and flat gold wires for the cloisons. Champlevé was also much used for religious enamels. The church art of the early nineteenth century continued to employ all of the traditional enamel techniques described and added to them the beautiful Limoges painter's technique.

The styles of church buildings in this period were an assortment of Romanesque, Gothic, Renaissance, and Baroque. In the nineteenth century there were new buildings constructed of new materials, such as iron and steel, glass and concrete, and new technical discoveries helped to promote their use. In the great present-day church building boom, both the architect and patron are becoming increasingly conscious of the truth that man is a creature of emotion as well as of intellect. There is growing recognition of the spiritual contribution that is made to the atmosphere of worship by the painter, the sculptor, the ceramist, the enamelist, the metal worker and the silversmith, all craftsmen working in close collaboration with the architect in solving difficult decorative problems.

My first experience with church enamels was in 1955 when, at the request of architect Ray J. Koski, my wife, Thelma, and I were invited to design and execute enameled steel mural decorations for the Bethany Evangelical Lutheran Church of Ashtabula, Ohio. Through Thelma Winter's knowledge of and interest in Biblical figures, she assumed the creative designing of these sectional decorations. In her design she used a system of dynamic symmetry that directed the eye of the observer to follow the lines of the horizontal and diagonals throughout all sections of the decoration.

The three panels shown above are over the central doors of the
Bethany Evangelical Lutheran Church in Ashtabula, Ohio. In the
illustration below, all nine of the 2 x 4½-foot panels are shown.

Vitreous enamel murals being installed over front doors of the Bethany Evangelical Lutheran Church at Ashtabula, Ohio.

The executing of the work was, of course, in my domain. Months were devoted to study and research of the apostles, their characters, facial expressions, costumes and other trappings so that they would be historically and technically correct. I employed a combination of several techniques: sgraffito, line drawing, gold inlay, painter's effects, crackle, and template. Each panel, which was 54-inches high, received approximately ten firings, each ranging from 1440°F. to 1500°F. By skillful handling and firing, the assorted colored enamels retained all of their strong color values. More than a year was needed to complete this eighteen-foot sectional decoration, the largest religious enamel produced to date.

Firing church panels at a furnace temperature of
1500°F. for a period of three minutes.

These are the raw materials used to make opaque enamel. They must be put into a smelter of 2300° F. for several hours until melted into liquid glass. This is then poured onto heavy steel slabs or into a tank of water to frit and cool.

RAW MATERIALS

All vitreous enamels are basically glass, and one of the principal constituents of glass is glass sand, or silica (SiO_2), Silica is found in a very pure state as soft sandstone near Ottawa, Illinois, and there is another very fine silica or quartz deposit near Lewiston, Pennsylvania. There are also some good glass sands in the New Jersey area, but they are not as pure as the sand from the first two sources mentioned. The sand used by the enamel manufacturer is first powdered to about 120 or 140-meshes or openings to the lineal inch. As there are 14,400 openings per square inch in such a fine screen, material passing through it is literally as fine as dust.

The next most important material that enters into the composition of the copper enamels is lead. Litharge (PbO), red lead (Pb_3O_4), and white lead or basic lead carbonate ($2PbCO_4$) and white lead or basic lead carbonate ($2PbCO_3\text{-}Pb(OH)_2$) are the three chemical forms of lead used. Borax ($Na_2B_4O_7$) and boric acid (H_3BO_3) are also essential ingredients of enamels. Both of these are excellent fluxes and glass-forming materials. Borax is found in native rock form in Death Valley and the Mojave Desert, as well as in the heavily concentrated

Opaque white enamel in large lumps, ground to 80 mesh and 200 mesh.

salt brine of Searless Lake in California where the purification and refining of the product is a large industry.

Potash or potassium carbonate (K_2CO_3) which is likewise used as a flux in enamels, formerly came from Germany, but within recent years large potash deposits have been discovered in New Mexico.

Feldspar is another complex silicate. It is used as a refractory in some enamels. Mineralogically, it is a potassium-sodium-aluminum-silicate. It is usually found in a rocky formation in Tennessee, North Carolina, North Dakota, and Maine, as well as in Arizona.

Bone ash or calcium phosphate ($Ca_3(PO_4)_2$) is used as an accessory opacifier, so-called because it assists the principal opacifiers in their function.

Sodium fluoride (NaF), which has recently been given some publicity as an additive to drinking water to help prevent tooth decay, is used in enamels to impart a milky opacity as well as for its fluxing action which helps dissolve the silica and feldspar and form a glass.

Arsenic trioxide (As_2O_3) is used in these lead-bearing enamels to obtain opacity. Because of its poisonous nature, it definitely cannot be tolerated in enamels made for cooking utensils, but its use is permissible in art and jeweler's enamels.

Titanium dioxide (TiO_2) is likewise an opacifier in enamels, and it is a useful ingredient to help develop acid resistance. Like silica and feldspar, it is a refractory. Certain sands in Florida are an important source of this material.

Color in enamels is produced by the addition of oxides of various metals. In order to promote transparency, the oxides are always smelted into the raw material batch. The metal oxides which are most frequently used, their source, and the color produced by their addition, is shown in the following table:

OXIDE	SOURCE	COLOR
Cobalt	Canada and Africa	Blue
Copper	Colorado, Utah, Mexico	Blue green

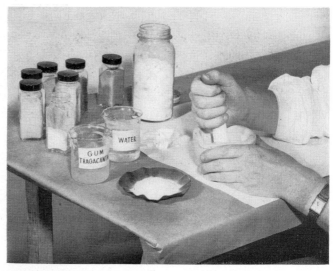

Enamel purchased in lump frit can be reduced to 80-mesh powder. After striking the hammer several times the contents can be put through an 80-mesh or 60-mesh sieve.

The large lumps of enamel should be broken down with the steel mortar and pestle, as shown in preceding picture; but if a paste made of 150- or 200-mesh powder is wanted the material can be ground in this porcelain mortar. A few drops of water and gum will aid in the grinding.

Chromium	Western States	Greens
Gold	Western States	Ruby and pink
Silver	Western States	Yellow
Manganese	Western States	Purples
Antimony	Western States	Yellows
Uranium	Canada (not available)	Yellows-reds
Iron oxide	Minnesota	Brown, black, and green
Nickel oxide	Canada	Gray and brown
Selenium	Western States	Red

The various ingredients necessary for each particular type of enamel are carefully weighed out according to predetermined formulae and melted in fire clay crucibles at a temperature in excess of 2000° F. for a period of several hours. The hardness or softness of various enamel compositions can be varied by changing the proportion of ingredients used in the mixture, and hundreds of color variations can be obtained in transparent and opaque colors by changing the amounts and combinations of the various metal oxides. For example, a typical flux (clear glass) or glaze formula would be: silica sand 34, lead oxide 50, potassium nitrate 7, sodium carbonate 8. Ingredients for an opaque enamel would be: silica sand 33, lead oxide 53, potassium nitrate 4, sodium carbonate 5, arsenic 5.

133

The lumps of frit can be ground into a fine powder by the use of a porcelain ball mill. The length of time depends upon the degree of fineness desired — anywhere from 3 to 4 hours for 80-mesh and 10-12 hours for 400-mesh.

PREPARING AND GRINDING ENAMELS

Enamels, both transparent and opaque, may be purchased from the manufacturer, crushed or ground into coarse or fine powder. For dry application through a sieve, enamels are usually ground to 80-mesh; that is, the enamel will pass through a screen with 80 openings to the lineal inch. Sometimes a coarser 60-mesh screen is used for cloisonné work. For fine enamel painting, a 200- to 400-mesh powder is used. This is comparable in fineness to face powder. Artists can grind their own enamels from lumps by placing the lumps in a steel mortar and hitting them with a hammer. A porcelain mortar can be used to grind a powder into an even finer state.

Large-scale enameling operations require ball mills for dry grinds or a huge crusher to reduce large lump enamel into smaller particles. In using a steel mortar it is advisable to run a magnet through your powdered enamel to pick up any small particles of steel that might have come from the mortar. Small particles of steel fired into the enamel will produce small black spots. Powdered enamel covered with clean water will keep quite satisfactorily for some time, and when it is required for use, the water is poured off and the enamel dried.

Washing transparent enamel powder. Although it is not always necessary to wash powdered enamel to remove the gray, cloudy silt that results from the grinding operation, washing does give an assurance that the enamel will come out clear and transparent after firing. Pour the powder into any suitable container and allow clean water to run into it, stirring gently so that the enamel itself does not drain off.

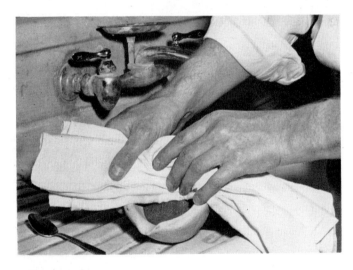

Drying is speeded up with the use of a dry towel before further drying in oven or over a hot plate. The enamel must be thoroughly dried to powder state before it is ready to use. It is not necessary to wash opaque enamels.

Luminous transparent enamel in lump form gives off a gem-like quality. After it is ground and dried it is ready for sifting onto the metal surface.

135

WASHING AND STORAGE OF ENAMELS

While the washing of enamel powders is not absolutely necessary today when there is so much cleanliness in their manufacture and grinding, it is sometimes advisable to wash them if particularly clear transparencies are required. To wash the enamel put some of the 80-mesh powder in a bowl (nickel or Pyrex if possible) and run some water into it. After a few stirrings with a glass rod or a spoon, a milky silt appears. Pour off this whitish water, being careful not to pour out the enamel as well. Repeat this three or four times until no further silt appears. Absorb moisture from the enamel with absorbent paper or a clean towel. It can be stirred up and heated slightly to hasten drying. When in a completely dry powdered state again, it is ready to use.

When enamels are to be stored for any length of time, it is advisable to buy them in lump form for stocking on the shelf. Powdered enamel, especially the transparent variety, does not keep too well over a period of several weeks or months due to absorption of moisture from the atmosphere. The gases in the air form chemical composition which attack the enamel. Ground or powdered enamels kept tight in a Mason jar with rubber rings can be protected from this atmospheric contamination. If unprotected for weeks, thousands of tiny pinholes will appear in the enameled surface when it is fired, spoiling its transparency and giving it a slightly opaque quality.

Enamels can be classified into three distinct types: opaque, transparent, and opalescent. No light can penetrate the opaques, only the surface will reflect light. Black, white, gray and, of course, most all colors are opaque. Transparent colored enamels are those through which a varying amount of light passes quite readily, depending upon their value—light, medium, or dark.

Opalescent or translucent enamels, as they are sometimes called, are similar to the transparent variety, but the transparency is slightly clouded by a milky veil which gives them a subtle and delicate quality. The word "translucid" is especially applied to plique-à-jour; that is, to enamel through which light passes freely as through a stained-glass window of a cathedral, heightening the play of color in the rich, transparent masses.

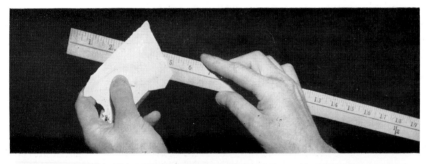

Opaque white enamels are of a solid substance through which no light can pass.

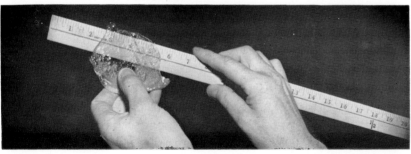

Ruler can be seen clearly through this piece of transparent enamel.

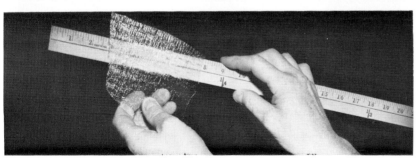

The ruler is only partly visible when seen through a piece of translucent enamel.

An adhesive binder must be used when finely ground enamel powder is being applied to metal surfaces. Oftentimes the beginner is inclined to apply these adhesives too thickly and heavily, killing the possibility of producing a transparent, clear color to the enamel and causing bubbles to appear when the enamel is melting. The gum application should be so thin and clear it looks almost like clear water.

Gum tragacanth, which is mostly used, is obtained from various species of astragalus, a shrub native to Asia Minor. It comes on the market (purchased in most drug stores) in dull, hard, crinkly, ribbon-like pieces, sometimes yellowish or grayish white. When soaked in water overnight, it swells into a gelatinous mass. By adding more water to it and cooking it, it becomes more fluid but still is a fairly colloidal solution. After cooling, more water can be added and the entire contents strained through cheesecloth, muslin, or a 200-mesh sieve.

Gum arabic or gum acacia is a product of various trees which grow in tropical Asia, Africa, and Australia, the best grades coming from Africa. The clean, pale varieties used in medicines and foods are best to use for an enamel binder. The preparation is the same as for gum tragacanth. Flake agar is used quite often as an adhesive but it does not have the holding power or adhesive qualities of tragacanth. Its preparation is similar to that of the other gums. If gums are applied too thickly or heavily, you will notice a dark brownish color when the enamel is entered into the furnace, although a slight brownish color is nothing to be alarmed about; it will burn away when the enamel reaches a high temperature.

In order to preserve solutions of gums and agars and keep them from decomposing through bacterial action or fermentation, a few drops of alcohol or a pinch of benzoate of soda will serve as preservatives. New types of adhesives occasionally appear on the market and can be experimented with by the craftsman.

While gum tragacanth is being cooked and dissolved, stir it occasionally with a spoon or glass rod to keep it from sticking to the bottom of the utensil.

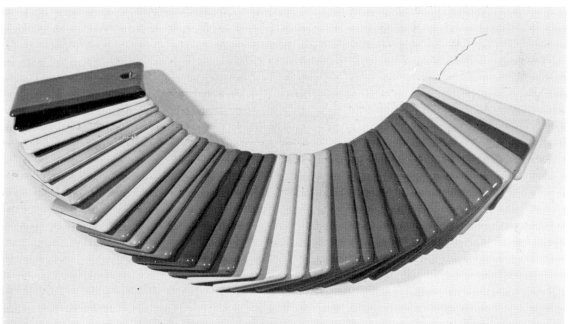

Making color samples. The craftsman should beat out long pieces of copper and drill a hole in their ends for the stringing together on a wire. Some pieces can have the assorted transparent colors applied to the copper itself and others can show color tones derived from transparent enamel applied and fired over an opaque white surface which has been previously fired. As many color samples as are desired can be made in this way.

Counterenamel refers to the enamel coating on the back or under-side of any piece. It must be remembered that under the influence of 1400° to 1500° temperature required to fuse enamel to metal, great expansion and contraction takes place. The copper expands to a greater degree than the enamel and, upon cooling, the metal contracts to a greater extent than the enamel. This produces a strain on a piece of metal—the larger the metal, the greater the strain—and this becomes evident either by the warping of the piece or a fracture of the enamel. To prevent this condition the metal should be enameled both front and back and thus help to keep the rigidity and form of the piece unaltered after firing. Even with counterenameled surfaces, large bowls and panels will come from the furnace red hot and in a slightly warped state. Wearing asbestos gloves to protect your hands, quickly pick up the piece and place it, rim down, on the cement floor or a rock-asbestos table top and press down upon it. This will assure its hardening in perfect shape.

Counterenameling is really an important, if somewhat difficult, procedure, because if only one side of a piece is enameled, the other side of the copper, unprotected, will scale off in firing; it will have to be thoroughly cleaned with acid or steel wool to make it receptive to enameling. Learning to do both sides at the same time, and then firing, will save much time and trouble.

FURNACES AND FIRING DEVICES

Through the centuries there have been four principal systems of firing enamel: the coke, the gas, the benzene, and the electric furnaces. The electric furnace, the easiest to operate, is inexpensive to run, completely clean, and maintains accurate temperature. It also produces a sharp heat and, with a pyrometer, will maintain any set temperature accurately. The best types of electric furnaces are those with heating elements on the bottom, sides, and top. Sharp, direct heat from the bottom produces better enameling results since the heat rises and heats the object more quickly.

All wire elements on the bottom of the furnace muffle should be covered with fire clay refractory to protect them from chance enamel drippings. This precaution is given for the benefit of those who make their own furnaces—commercially made furnaces are always mechanically perfect. There are many fine enameling furnaces of all sizes and

TOOLS FOR SIMPLE METAL FORMING

1. Emery cloth, coarse and fine. 2. Carborundum or rubbing stone, medium grade. 3. Small table vice for holding stake and hammers. 4. Hard steel stake (planishing half-round). 5. Tinning shears, medium size. 6. Planishing hammer. 7. Flat-edge medium file.

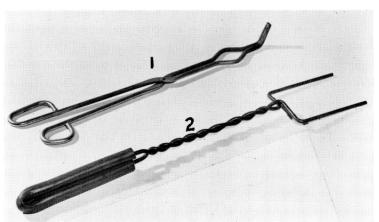

1. Large crucible nickel tongs are used to grab wire screen or planch in placing enamels in the furnace and removing them. A long tool enables one to operate at a comfortable distance from the furnace heat. 2. Long chromel round wire fork. The rubber tubing keeps it from burning the hands.

One of the most effective and easy to make supports for firing small pieces is made of a 5-inch square of 20-gauge chromel metal. The center is cut out and the piece bent up as shown. It can be used for hand-torch or furnace firing with or without a screen.

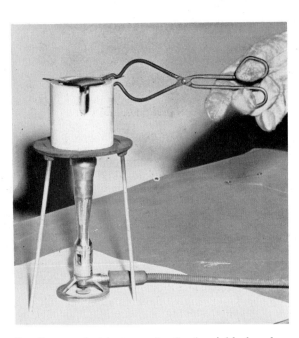

Small enamel objects can be fired quickly by placing them on a chromel triangle wire inserted in top of clay furnace. The piece is removed with tongs. The same kind of furnace can be used in firing small jewelry items, using a propane torch from the underside of the piece.

The fire-clay furnace is a cylinder 3¾ inches long by 3½ inches in diameter. The wall is about ½-inch thick. When placed on top of a steel tripod with a burner or torch playing from beneath, the clay walls create an intense heat that quickly melts the enamel resting upon the chromel triangle. The wire rests in the three indentations of the cylinder. Care must be taken with this cylinder to prevent its cracking or breaking.

Firing supports of various kinds. Trivets, chromel wire screen, and fire-clay triangles and stilts are used to hold enamel while in the furnace. Chromel trivets support the piece to be fired without showing marks on the underside. The short and long tongs are used to place work in the furnace.

prices on the market. Enameling furnaces can be used to fire pottery, but unfortunately pottery kilns are not too suitable for firing enamels. The clay refractory walls are usually different in these two types of furnaces.

Enameling furnaces have doors that open easily and, at the same time, do not allow too much heat to escape. The size of the furnace depends upon the size and quantity of work that is to be fired. A good size for school or laboratory with a door opening of seven to eight-inches wide and about five or six-inches high may cost from thirty to fifty dollars. For classrooms, where many students want to use the furnace, it is advisable to have two or three of the same size and then students can sign up and take turns getting their work fired. Most furnaces come with built-in pyrometer for a temperature gauge, but in-

143

Wide spatulas are indispensable for handling and straightening objects just removed from the furnace. Cotton gloves should be worn for safety.

It is advisable to have an "interval timer" for timing enamels in the furnace. An alarm bell rings when the time is up. This type of clock is made by the General Electric Co.

dividual pyrometers can be purchased and connected to any furnace.

The success or failure of good enameling depends in great measure on the precision with which work is fired. The old gas and coke furnaces gave off a peculiar atmosphere in the muffle of the furnaces which sometimes produced a reducing quality to some enamels. The automatic propane hand torch, which has been on the market a short time, is adequate for small pieces of jewelry, buttons, and other craft items. It contains a refrigerant gas, a liquefier petroleum product, whiich gives a quick over-all heat. It is available at all hardware and department stores. It is clean and of superior quality. Unlike the old torches that had to be filled, primed and pumped, this master torch eliminates filling and spilling. Lightweight and compact, the Bernz-o-matic torch, when assembled, weighs less than three pounds, and may be held for long periods without tiring the arm. It fits neatly into a pocket, toolbox, or drawer and needs no tangling hose and bulky tank or bellows.

This burner comes in two sections, a brass burner and a fuel cylinder. The flame burner screws into the top of the cylinder with a twist of the hand. These cylinders contain enough fuel for weeks of normal use. They are disposable when the fuel is exhausted and new ones can

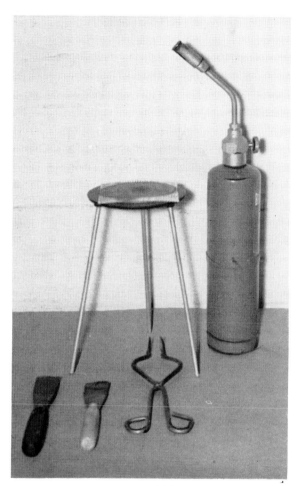

The propane hand torch can be used in fusing enamel or small pieces. The tripod legs screw into ring top that supports a wire screen made of chromel wire which does not scale under intense heat.

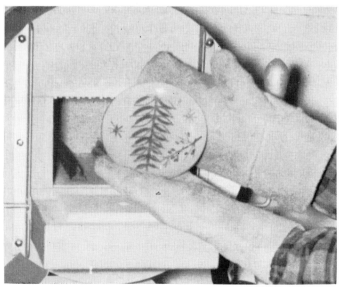

Heavy asbestos mittens are essential to protect the hands when handling the piece while it is hot. In a classroom several pairs of mittens should be provided for students' use. In addition, soft finger gloves should be available for handling pieces when still warm though not hot enough to require the heavier asbestos gloves. Pieces that come from the furnace in a slightly warped condition can often be straightened by picking them off the trivet and placing them on an unburnable surface with the asbestos gloves. An enamel fresh from the furnace should loose its bright red glow before it is handled with the asbestos mittens.

145

Round-face planishing stake is 5½ inches in diameter, having a surface radius of 5 inches. It is used for forming and planishing large ash trays and bowls. The flat planishing stake of 4-inch diameter is used for planishing flat or shallow surfaces of medium sized trays, bottoms of dishes, etc.

be purchased at a nominal cost. The brass burner nozzle can be retained and used indefinitely. Complete directions go with each burner. The torch can be used for drying out any moisture in the enamel by playing the flame to the underside very lightly. It should be held close to the underside of the enamel for successful enamel fusion. The torch is also good for soldering.

The fire clay cylinder, or tube furnace as it is sometimes called, sits on a metal tripod over a Fisher-type Bunsen burner and the small enamel piece that is to be fired is placed within the cylinder on a chrome triangle as illustrated. The propane hand torch will also give off more heat if it is played into the cylinder from the underside. These different firing devices are illustrated because one manner of firing enamels may appear more exciting to one person than another, each one having its own fascination.

MATERIALS AND WHERE TO BUY THEM

ADHESIVES
Miracle Adhesive Corp., 214 East 53rd St., New York 22, N. Y.

ENAMELS
FOR ALUMINUM
E. I. Du Pont de Nemours & Co., Electrochemicals Dept., Wilmington, Del.
Ferro Corp., 4150 East 56th St., Cleveland 5, Ohio.
Pemco Corp., Baltimore, Md.

FOR COPPER, GOLD, SILVER, AND CAST IRON
Allcraft Tool and Supply Co., 11 East 48th St., New York 17, N. Y.
American Art Clay Co., Indianapolis, Ind.
Carpenter & Wood, Providence, R. I.
B. F. Drakenfeld & Co., 45 Park Place, New York 7, N. Y.
Enamel-Craft Co., University Center Station, Box 1940, Cleveland 6, Ohio.
Products of the Universe, Box 8, Swiss Division, Universal City, Calif.
The Thomas C. Thompson Co., 1539 Deerfield Rd., Highland Park, Ill.
S. Paul Ward Co., 601 Mission St., So. Pasadena, Calif.
Wengers, Ltd., Etruria, Stoke on Trent, England.

FOR IRON AND STEEL
Ceramic Color & Mfg. Co., New Brighton, Penn.
Chicago Vitreous Enameling Co., Cicero, Ill.
Enamel-Craft Co., University Center Station, Box 1940, Cleveland 6, Ohio.
Harshaw Chemical Co., 1945 East 97th St., Cleveland 6, Ohio.
O. Hommel Co., Pittsburgh 30, Penna.
Pemco Corp., Baltimore, Md.
Vitro Mfg. Co., Corliss Station, Pittsburgh 4, Penna.

FURNACES — ENAMELING
Dickinson Pottery Equipment Co., 2424 Glover Pl., Los Angeles, Calif.
Electric Hotpack Co., Coltman Ave. at Melrose St., Philadelphia, Penna.
Ferro Corp., 4150 East 56th St., Cleveland 5, Ohio.
Hevi-Duty Electric Co., 4212 Highland Ave., Milwaukee, Wisc.
O. Hommel Co., Pittsburgh 30, Penna.
Hoskins Mfg. Co., 4435 Lawton Ave., Detroit 8, Mich.
L & L Mfg. Co., 804 Mulberry St., Upland (Chester), Penna.
Pereny Equipment Co., Dept. C, 893 Chambers Rd., Columbus, Ohio.
Swindell-Dressler Corp., P.O. Box 1888, Pittsburgh, Penna.
James W. Weldon Co., 2315 Harrison Ave., Kansas City 8, Mo.

GLOVES
The Des Moines Mfg. Co., Des Moines, Iowa.
Any hardware store.

GOLD FOIL
Hastings & Co., 2314 Market St., Philadelphia 3, Penna.
Wehrung & Billmeier Co., 3624-26 Lincoln Ave., Chicago, Ill.

JEWELRY FINDINGS
Bergen Arts & Crafts, Dept. CBE, 128 Main St., Hackensack, N. Y.
The Copper Shop, 1812 East 13th St., Cleveland, Ohio.
Enamel-Craft Co., University Center Station, Box 1940, Cleveland 6, Ohio.
T. B. Hagstoz & Co., 707 Sansom St., Philadelphia 6, Penna.
Metal Findings Corp., 150 West 22nd St., New York 11, N. Y.

LUSTERS
D. M. Campana Art Co., 442 No. Wells St., Chicago 10, Ill.
Hanovia Chemical Co., Chestnut St. & New Jersey Railroad, Newark, N. J.
Harshaw Chemical Co., 1945 East 97th St., Cleveland 6, Ohio.

METALS

ALUMINUM

Aluminum Co. of America, ALCOA Building, Pittsburgh, Penna. (Offices in most cities.)

Reynolds Metals Co., So. Third St., Louisville, Ky. (Offices in most cities.)

Suppliers in most cities.

COPPER

The American Brass Co., Waterbury, Conn. (Offices in most cities.)

Chase Brass & Copper Co. (Offices in most cities.)

SILVER

Handy & Harmon, 82 Fulton St., New York 38, N. Y.

STEEL AND IRON

American Rolling Mill, Middletown, Ohio. (Offices in most cities.)

Inland Steel Co., 38 So. Dearborn St., Chicago, Ill.

SILVER FOIL

J. M. Ney & Co., 71 Elm St., Hartford, Conn.

Wehrung & Billmeier Co., 3624-26 Lincoln Ave., Chicago, Ill.

STILTS AND TRIVOTS

Artex Mfg. Co., 4038 Huron Ave., Culver City, Calif.

Atlas Steel Point Stilt Co., 4207 Longshore St., Philadelphia 35, Penna.

Charles H. Draving Co., P. O. Box 26, Feasterville, Penna.

The Potters Supply Co., East Liverpool, Ohio.

TEXTURE MATERIALS

Enamel-Craft Co., University Center Station, Box 1940, Cleveland 6, Ohio.

TOOLS AND EQUIPMENT

Allcraft Tool & Supply Co., 11 East 48th St., New York 17, N. Y.

Anchor Tool & Supply Co., 12 John St., New York 7, N. Y.

Brodhead & Garrett, 4560 East 71st St., Cleveland, Ohio.

William Dixon, Inc., 32-42 East Kinney St., Newark, N. J.

George H. Fuller & Sons Co., 29 East Madison Ave., Chicago, Ill.

Paul H. Gessewein & Co., 35 Maiden Lane, New York 38, N. Y.

Ohio Jewelers Supply Co., 1000 Schofield Building, Cleveland 15, Ohio.

TORCHES AND BURNERS

The Otto Bernz Co., 280 Lyell Ave., Rochester 6, N. Y.

Enamel-Craft Co., University Center Station, Box 1940, Cleveland 6, Ohio.

Hardware and Department Stores.

BIBLIOGRAPHY

Addison, Julia DeWolf, *Arts and Crafts in the Middle Ages*. Boston, L. C. Page & Co., 1908.

Andrews, A. I. *Enamels*. Champaign, Ill., Garrard Press, 1936.

Bates, Kenneth F., *Enameling, Principles and Practice,* Cleveland, World Publishing Co., 1951.

Brown, W. N., *The Art of Enameling*. London, Scott, Greenwood & Co., 1900.

Bryant, Eugene E., *Porcelain Enameling Operations*. Cleveland, Enamelist Publishing Co., 1953.

Cleveland Museum of Art, *Bulletin*. May 1933.

Cunnynghame, H. H., *The Art of Enameling Metal*. Westminster, England, Archibald Constable & Co., Ltd., 1899.

De Koningh, H., *The Preparation of Precious and Other Metals for Enameling*. New York, The Norman W. Henley Publishing Co., 1930.

Encyclopaedia Britannica, Vol. 8, "Enamel."

Feirer, John L., *Modern Metalcraft,* Peoria, Ill., The Manual Arts Press, 1946.

Fisher, Alexander, *The Art of Enameling on Metal*. London, The Studio, 1906.

Hart, G. F., and Golden Keeley, *Metal Work for Craftsmen*. London, Sir Isaac & Sons, Ltd., 1945.

Landrum, R. D., *Enamels*. Cleveland, Harshaw Chemical Co., Inc., 1918.

Larom, Mary, *Enameling for Fun and Profit*. New York, David McKay Co., 1954.

Lehnert, Georg Hermann, ed., *Illustrierte Geschichte des Kunstgewerbeschule,* Vol. 1. Berlin, M. Oldenbourg, 1907.

Martin, Charles J., *How to Make Modern Jewelry*. New York, Simon & Schuster, 1949.

Metropolitan Museum of Art, *Bulletin,* "Masterpieces of Enameling." New York, Metropolitan Museum of Art, May 1940.

Millenet, Louis Elie, and H. DeKoningh, *Enameling on Metal*. London, Crosby Lockwood & Sons, 1926.

Miller, John G., *Metal Art Crafts*. New York, D. Van Nostrand Co., 1948.

Morgan, J. Pierpont, *Catalogue of the Collections of Jewels and Precious Works of Art*. London, Chiswisk Press, 1910.

Neuburger, Albert, *The Technical Arts and Sciences of the Ancients*. New York, MacMillan Co., 1930.

Otten, Mizi, and Kathe Berle, *The Art of Enameling Can Be Fun*. New York, 1950.

Pack, Greta, *Jewelry and Enameling*. New York, D. Van Nostrand Co., 1941.

Rosenthal, Rudolf, and Helen L. Ratzka, *The Story of Modern Applied Art*. New York, Harper & Bros., 1948.

Stuckert, L., *Die Emailfabrikation,* 1929.

Thompson, Thomas E., *Enameling on Copper and Other Metals*. Thomas C. Thompson Co., 1950.

University of Pittsburgh, Department of Fine Arts, *Catalogue of Exhibition,* "History of Enamels." Pittsburgh, University of Pittsburgh, Apr. 8, 1950.

Untracht, Oppi, *Enameling on Metal*. New York, Greenberg, 1957.

Weaver, Robert A., *An Ancient Art Becomes a Modern Industry*. 1934.

Wiener, Louis, *Hand Made Jewelry*. New York, D. Van Nostrand Co., 1948.

Winebrenner, D. Kenneth, *Jewelry Making as an Art Expression*. Scranton, International Textbook Co., 1953.

Winter, Edward, *Porcelain Enamel Art for Beginners*. Cleveland, Enamelist Publishing Co., 1947.

MAGAZINE ARTICLES BY THE AUTHOR

American Architect Magazine, Jan. 1934.

American Artist, Oct. 1941, Dec. 1941, Sept. 1947, May 1953, Apr. 1956.

American Ceramic Society Bulletin, May 1948, Apr. 1949, Oct. 1952.

American Magazine of Art, Apr. 1933, June 1933, June 1934, Sept. 1934, June 1936, Sept. 1938, July 1939, June 1940.

Architectural Forum, Feb. 1934, Apr. 1941, Sept. 1951.

Architectural League of New York, Gold Medal Award Catalogue 1953, Honorable Mention.

Art Digest and the Arts, Feb. 1954, June 1956.

Art in Focus, Apr. 1952, Feb. 1954.

Art News, Oct. 1936, May 1938, Sept. 1951.

Arts and Decoration, Jan. 1939.

Better Homes and Gardens, Dec. 1947.

Bachelor Magazine, Oct. 1937.

Better Enameling, May 1935.

Building Research Institute, Nov. 1953.

Business Week, Sept. 1953.

Bystander Magazine, Oct. 1932, Aug. 1933, Nov. 1933.

California Arts and Architecture, Oct. 1936.

Central Glass and Ceramic Research Institute, Calcutta, India, Vol. 4, No. 1, 1957.

Ceramic Age, Feb. 1934, Mar. 1935, Jan. 1941, July 1951, Aug. 1951, Sept. 1951, Feb. 1952, Dec. 1952, Aug. 1953, Sept. 1953, Apr. 1954, May 1954, Jan. 1955, May 1955, Feb. 1956.

Ceramic Industry, Mar. 1934, Sept. 1940, June 1941, Feb. 1945, Aug. 1945, Aug. 1946, June 1947, Sept. 1947, July 1950, May 1951, Oct. 1951, Jan. 1952, Apr. 1952, July 1952, Dec. 1952, Oct. 1953, May 1954, Apr. 1955, Apr. 1956.

Church Management, Apr. 1956.

Clevelander Magazine, May 1935, June 1937, Mar. 1950.

Commercial Art and Industry, London, England, Mar. 1935.

Country Life and the Sportsman, Dec. 1937.

Crockery and Glass Journal, Feb. 1940.

Cross Country Craftsman, Oct. 1951, Dec. 1955.

Decorative Art Golden Gate Exposition, 1939.

Design Magazine, June 1933, June 1935, Nov. 1936, Feb. 1937, Apr. 1937, May 1937, Nov. 1937, Feb. 1942, Apr. 1947, Apr. 1948, May 1950, Oct. 1951, Dec. 1951, Jan. 1952, Dec. 1953, Jan. 1954, Feb. 1954, Nov. 1954, Mar. 1955, Apr. 1955, Nov. 1955, May 1957.

Du Pont Magazine, June 1954.

Emaillerie Magazine, Paris, France, Oct. 1935, May 1936.

The Enamelist, May 1933, June 1933, Aug. 1933, Sept. 1933, Mar. 1934, Apr. 1934, July 1934, Nov. 1934, June 1935, Jan. 1936, May 1936, July 1936, Mar. 1937, June 1938, Sept. 1938, Jan. 1939, May 1939, Feb. 1940, May 1941, July 1941, Oct. 1941, June 1947, Jan. 1949.

Engineering Experiment Station News, Oct. 1947.

Finish Magazine, June 1945, June 1946, July 1947, Jan. 1948, June 1948, Apr. 1948, Aug. 1948, May 1951, Oct. 1951, May 1952, Oct. 1953, Aug. 1955.

Gift and Art Buyer, Mar. 1940, May 1940, June 1940, Oct. 1940, Nov. 1940, Aug. 1941, Feb. 1947, May 1947, June 1947, Aug. 1947, Feb. 1948, June 1948, July 1948, Jan. 1951, July 1951, Dec. 1952, Oct. 1953, Apr. 1954, May 1954, July 1955, Jan. 1957, July 1957, Oct. 1957, Jan. 1958.

House and Garden, Nov. 1940.

Industrial Finishing, July 1934.

Interiors, Aug. 1953.

Iron Age, Feb. 1934, July 1941.

Jewelers Circular Keystone, May 1940.

London Studio, 1932.

Los Angeles Times Magazine, Jan. 1936

Materials and Methods, Dec. 1953.

McGraw Hill Digest, Sept. 1952, Dec. 1953.

Modern Homes and Gardens, Jan. 1935.

Modern Lamp Accessories, June 1952.

Modern Metals, Nov. 1936, Dec. 1937, Dec. 1950, Oct. 1952.

New Yorker, Dec. 2, 1950, Dec. 7, 1957.

New York Times Magazine, July 1934, Oct. 1937.

Office Management and Equipment, Nov. 1949, Jan. 1952.

Pacific Coast Ceramic News, Feb. 1955, Sept. 1955, Oct. 1955.

Pictures on Exhibit, June 1955, June 1956.

Plain Dealer Pictorial Magazine, May 1937, Nov. 1951, Sept. 1953, Jan. 1955.

Popular Mechanics, May 1933, July 1941.

Popular Science, Dec. 1933, May 1954.

Porcelain Enamel Art for Beginners, Apr. 1947.

Pottery and Glass Salesman, Oct. 1941.

Public Works Magazine, Jan. 1958.

Screen Process Magazine, Nov. 1953, May 1955.

Signs of the Times, Sept. 1936, Aug. 1941, Sept. 1941, Dec. 1941, May 1944, Mar. 1948, Nov. 1951, Jan. 1953, Dec. 1953, May 1955, Apr. 1956.

Steel Magazine, Apr. 1932, Apr. 1934, June 1941.

Steelways, Mar. 1948.

Syracuse Herald Magazine, Nov. 20, 1933.

Today Philadelphia Inquirer Magazine, Dec. 9, 1951.

Today's America Magazine, Mar. 1934.

Town Tidings, Oct. 1932, Nov. 1932.

ABRASIVE. — A material used in grinding and polishing, such as emery or carborundum. Fine sand and pumice powder can be used to polish any metal previous to enameling.

ABSORBENT. — Cloth or paper towels serve to remove moisture from powdered enamel frit after washing, quickening the drying time.

ACID. — Used to etch or pickle metals.

ACID CROCK. — A glazed, covered jar for keeping sulphuric acid and water for pickling metal.

ACID-PROOF. — An enamel is considered acid-proof if, after being exposed to the action of a 10% citric acid solution for fifteen minutes, no shadow or stain can be seen. Enamels of this type are rated "Class AA" in acid resistance, since they are "stainless."

ACID-RESISTANT. — An enamel is considered acid-resistant if, after being exposed to the action of 10% citric acid solution for fifteen minutes, its surface has not been etched or made "chalky." Such enamels will show a "stain" and are rated "Class A" acid-resistant enamels. Most jeweler's or copper enamels are not acid-resistant, due to their high lead content.

ADHERENCE. — The property of an enamel that enables it to stick to, or bond with, a given metal surface.

AERATE. — To impregnate with a gas such as air or carbon dioxide. Sometimes refers to the purging of the enamel furnace atmosphere by the introducion of air into the burning chamber.

AGAR. — A vegetable gum solution used as a binder on metal to hold the powdered enamels when dusted on. Usually applied with camel's-hair brush in a thinned, watery state. Boiled in water.

ALLOY. — An intimate combination of metals, usually produced by fusion. In enameling, special alloys are used for burning equipment, such as racks and trivets to hold objects while in the furnace. Nickel is used, as it does not scale off and mar the ware being fired.

ALUMINA (aluminum oxide). — The oxide of aluminum metal. This oxide forms readily on the surface of pure aluminum and acts as a protective coating, in that it prevents further oxidation of the metal. Alumina is present in clays and feldspar. It is also found in a pure state in nature as corundum, ruby and sapphire stones. Alumina exists in most enamels and is generally introduced into enamel frit compositions as feldspar or aluminum hydrate.

AMORPHOUS. — Noncrystalline. Materials like borax, feldspar, and quartz are crystalline, but the glass derived from melting mixtures of the three is amorphous. Many glasses and enamels are completely amorphous.

ANHYDROUS. — A compound which has lost all its water; for example, dehydrated borax (used as flux for silver soldering) in lump or powdered form.

ANNEAL. — To temper by heating and subsequent cooling. To burn off grease and other foreign matter on sheet copper before pickling. Aluminum, as well as cast iron, are annealed previous to enamel application; from 1200°F. to 1600°F for cast iron, and approximately five to six minutes at 1000°F. for sheet aluminum.

ANODE. — The positive terminal, pole, or electrode of an electric source. Found in all electric enameling furnaces.

ANTIMONY. — An element of the arsenic or nitrogen family. Used in copper enamels and some steel enamels. Also found in many soft alloys.

ANTIMONY OXIDE. — Oxide used as an opacifier in the making of enamels.

ARSENIC. — An element of the phosphorous group used in copper and jewelry enamels.

ASBESTOS. — A fibrous variety of amphibole distinguished by its ability to resist high temperatures and the action of acids and capable of being spun and woven. Most asbestos comes from the Province of Quebec, Canada. Used for aprons and mitts for enameling.

ASPHALTUM. — A black tar composition used to paint on metal as an acid resist.

ATMOSPHERE CONTROL. — An effort to control the gases inside the burning chamber by evacuation of objectionable gases present and the introduction of desired gases. For reduction purposes, etc.

BALL MILL. — A rotating cylindrical grinding mill wherein enamel frit is wet or dry-ground, using pebbles or porcelain balls as grinding media.

BASSE-TAILLE ENAMELING. — A type of art enameling in which the artist first carves the subject in low relief, usually on silver, and then covers this with a transparent or translucent enamel which, after fusing, is level with the uncarved part. The contours and third-dimension of the design show through the transparent enamel.

BAUXITE. — One of the chief sources of aluminum. The mineral bauxite is hydrated alumina.

BELLOWS. — Foot bellows, for pumping air when using a hand torch for firing enamels or soldering metal parts.

BLANK. — A term widely used in sheet metal working to denote the piece that is used in forming the finished article. The operation which consists of punching or cutting the blanks from the original sheet of metal, such as die stamping or metal spinning.

BLASTING. — Cleaning of metal surfaces by means of an abrasive projected by compressed air. Used to roughen a copper surface in contrast to smooth part as section of design pattern, then enameled with transparent enamel. Cast iron is cleaned this way before enameling.

BLISTERS. — A bubble-like appearance on the surface of enamel. Generally the result of gas evolution while the enamel is molten. Bubbles often caused by defective copper with an over amount of zinc content. Bubbles appear upon second firing when the gases under fired enamel are trying to escape.

BLOWPIPE. — Used to hold in the hand and train heat on an object to be fired.

BOND. — A term referring to the adhesive properties of an enamel.

BONE ASH. — Calcium phosphate, often used as an opacifier in the manufacturing of enamels.

BORAX. — Crystalline sodium borate. Refined from native rock found in western states. Used as a raw material in enamel and glass manufacturing.

BRIGHT DIP. — A solution of equal parts of sulphuric and nitric acid with the addition of a few grains of sodium chloride (table salt) added to water. It gives brightness to final pickling of copper before enameling.

BUBBLE STRUCTURE. — Refers to the existence of bubbles or blobs in the fused enamel. This structure is easily visible under a low-power magnifying glass. In general, transparent enamels have few bubbles (unless powdered frit is old).

BUFFING WHEEL. — A high-speed wheel of cloth, wool, felt, or rubber used to polish metal surfaces.

BURNER. — A device for obtaining a flame by the combustion of fuel. Gas and oil burners are most common.

BURNING. — Process of fusing vitreous enamels onto the metal base.

BURNING BARS. — Equipment usually of heat-resisting alloy construction, used for suspending or supporting articles during enamel fusion. Racks and trivets can be purchased or made up in any size to support objects while in the furnace. Heavy sheet nickel is usually used because it doesn't scale off.

BURNING-TOOL MARKS. — Defects in an enamel surface caused by trivet or burning tools in contact with the enamel article during firing.

CARBORUNDUM. — A trade name for synthetic silicon carbide used in refractories and as an abrasive in stoning edges of fired enamel to remove fired enamel from the edge of a bowl or any surface where it is not wanted.

CAUSTIC SODA. — Commercial sodium hydroxide. A strong alkali used in cleaning compounds for metals.

CERAMICS. — The science of dealing with inorganic substances such as clay, sand, limestone, and feldspar. The enamel (art and industrial) glass and structural clay products industries are important divisions of the ceramic industry.

CERAMIST. — A person trained or skilled in the field of ceramics, particularly ceramic or enamel art.

CHAMPLEVÉ ENAMELING. — A traditional method of enameling in which the design is cut into the metal base to some depth, and where two enamel colors meet there is a thin partition of the metal left to prevent the colors from running into each other when fusing.

CHARGING FORK. — Mechanical or hand fork for inserting the load or piece to be fired into a box-type enameling furnace.

CHIPPING. — A breaking off of enameled surface in flakes of various sizes; usually caused by enamels that don't fit the metal, or by dropping an already fired piece of ware.

CHROMEL. — A heat-resisting nickel chromium alloy used for burning supports, trivets, racks, and bars.

CLOISONNÉ ENAMELING. — A traditional technique where enamel is inlaid between partitions of bent copper, brass, silver, gold or steel wire attached to a metal base or fused into a prefired enamel surface. The flat-edged wires (of most any thickness) produce the desired pattern and keep the colors from running into each other in fusing. Upon completion, the top surface is stoned off with water to brighten the wires. A last, short firing restores the high gloss to the enamel, and buffing with a cloth wheel completes the process.

COBALT. — An element of the iron group. It is a steel gray, pinkish metal prepared by reduction of oxides by hydrogen gas. Produces blue color in transparent and opaque enamels. Used in combination with copper to produce black.

COEFFICIENT OF EXPANSION. — A value denoting the rate at which a material expands per unit of temperature rise.

COLLOID. — A state of subdivision of matter which consists of either single large molecules or of aggregations of smaller molecules. These particles of ultra-microscopic size may be solid, liquid, or gaseous and are surrounded by different matter which may also be solid, liquid or gaseous. Colloidal particles are subject to flocculation and deflocculation. Colloidal properties in a ruby or oxblood transparent enamel. Minute particles suspended in liquid gold and other lusters.

COLOR SCALE OF TEMPERATURE. — A visual scale of temperature. Incipient red heat: 500-600°C.; 932-1112°F. Dark red heat: 600-800°C.; 1112-1472°F. Bright red heat: 800-1000°C.; 1472-1832°F. Yellowish red heat: 1000-1200°C.; 1832-2192°F. Incipient white heat: 1200-1400°C.; 2192-2552°F. White heat: 1400-1600°C.; 2552-2912°F.

COMPLEMENTARY COLORS. — Any two colors of the spectrum which produce white light when combined or blended together as colored light.

CONSISTENCY. — The properties of a powdered enamel; fine or coarse grinding which enable it to pass through mesh sieve openings, such as 80-mesh grind for an 80-mesh sieve.

CONTAMINATION. — The introduction of foreign matter, dirt, dust, scale at any stage of the enameling process.

COPAIBA BALSAM—An oleoresin from various leguminous trees of tropical America. Used in paste and painting enamels.

COPPER ENAMEL. — An enamel designed for application to prepared copper surfaces containing properties that best fit the metal.

COPPER OXIDE. — A black powder used as a coloring agent in the manufacture of black or green enamels.

COUNTERENAMEL. — The enamel used on the reverse side of a piece to counteract the coefficient of expansion when it is fused several times. All metals and all objects if properly made must be counterenameled, adding to the serviceability and wearing qualities of the piece. Counterenameling prevents small and large pieces from warping and losing shape from the intense heat of the furnace.

COVER COAT. — The top or last coat of enamel applied to an object, as distinguished from the first, or base coat.

CRACKING. — Refers to the breaking of the fused enamel surface into small cracks when it is re-entered into the furnace heat. Such cracks fuse together after two minutes of fusion. Rough handling, bending or placing stress on a fired object will cause it to crack.

CRAWLING. — A condition very similar to "tearing" which occurs if a piece is being fired that isn't perfectly dried out or when there is too heavy an application of enamel.

CRIMPING. — An operation wherein the metal around or along the edge of a piece is shaped into the form of a roll or curl. Hand-hammered crinkle-edge ash trays or bowls. By beating or hammering the copper into a concave surface on top of a wood log or metal form.

CRUCIBLE. — For smelting raw materials into enamels or melting lump enamel to produce strings or threads.

DE-ENAMEL. — Removing enamel from a metal, as by sandblasting or in solution in a hot alkali bath.

DEFECTS. — Imperfections. Objectionable blemishes in an enamel surface, such as a pit, blister, scale or black speck in a white or colored surface. Unintended white specks appearing in black or dark colored surfaces.

DEGREASING. — Process of removing grease or dirt from metal, either by heating or immersion in hot alkali solutions.

DETERGENT. — A cleaning material.

DIES. — Any of the various tools used to impart a desired shape or form to a material. The dies used for drawing and stamping copper blanks for enameling are made of chilled, hardened tool steel. They vary in size and weight.

DIVIDERS. — A metal instrument for compassing circles in enamel surface.

DRAWING PENCIL. — "Ceramic," to produce white lines or drawings on dark fired enamel surface; does not burn away. Used for drawing and inlay technique.

DRIERS. — Heated compartments designed to remove water from damp enamel pieces before they are fired.

DRY PROCESS ENAMELING. — Refers to cast iron, copper or aluminum application, wherein powdered enamel is dusted onto metal surfaces with a sieve, as in art application.

DUSTING. — Dry process enameling. Applying with fine mesh sieve, powder used in fine ground state (100- to 200-mesh).

EAR WIRES. — Findings for earrings of assorted types.

EMBOSS. — To decorate, ornament or reinforce with raised surfaces. Usually effected by stamping in metal.

EMERY. — Granular variety of corundum used as an abrasive in grinding or polishing.

EMERY CLOTH. — For smoothing and polishing metals; fine and coarse.

ENAMELING IRON. — Sheet iron, suitable for vitreous enameling, must be either low-carbon steel or open hearth iron.

ENAMELWARE. — The products of the kitchenware industry are commonly referred to as enamelware.

ETCHED. — Enamel surfaces so affected by acid, alkalies, or other chemicals. Metals receive etched designs before transparent enamel application. Lines visible through the enamel.

FABRICATE. — To assemble, construct or manufacture.

FAHRENHEIT. — A thermometer scale invented by Gabriel Daniel Fahrenheit, a German physicist. On this scale water freezes at 32 degrees and boils at 212 degrees. One degree C. (centigrade) equals 1.8 degrees F.

FELDSPAR. — A mineral, known as potash spar, used as a refractory in the making of enamel.

FILES. — Assorted fine and coarse for metal working.

FINDINGS. — All forms of metal parts that can be used or incorporated in jewelry and other metal working shapes. Unusual in shape and design. Needle, pin backs, hooks, fastenings, chains, bezels and a thousand and one other similar items manufactured for and by jewelers for the artist and craftsman.

FINENESS OF ENAMEL. — The degree to which an enamel frit has been ground. For usual art application 60- 80- 100- and 200-mesh variety per square inch. (Mesh refers to the openings in a metal sieve.)

FIRING. — A term used as a synonym for burning. The process of fusing an enamel.

FRIT. — Small friable pieces of enamel glass produced by discharging molten enamel from the smelter or pot smelt into tanks containing water, thus quenching and shattering it. Lump frit is made by pouring out the molten enamel onto slabs of smooth steel to cool. Transparent enamels will retain their transparency and brilliance forever if left in this large lump state. Transparent enamels in powder form should not be kept too long before using; minute bubbles and cloudy appearance often form in enamels kept in the powder state too long.

FRITTING. — The process of quenching and shattering molten glass into small friable particles.

FURNACE. — The types and capacities of furnaces for enameling are numerous. There are small and large box types suitable for both studio and industrial uses, full muffle, semimuffle and continuous. Fuels commonly used are coal, gas, oil, and electricity.

FUSIBILITY. — The property of solid matter in becoming liquid on heating.

FUSION. — In enameling, fusion refers to the use of heat to effect the union or blending of enameling ingredients with the base metal or with previously fired enamel coating.

FUSION POINT. — The degree of heat at which any substance begins to melt or liquefy.

GASSY. — A furnace may become "gassy" through leaks in the muffle which allow gaseous products of combustion to enter the burning chamber. This can cause blisters in some opaque enamels; it has a tendency to make a smoky or fogged appearance on a transparent enamel surface. Opalescent effects often result when using an opaque enamel with a strong transparent base frit. This atmospheric effect can produce beautiful results not to be duplicated in clean electric furnaces.

GAUGE. — Also gage. An instrument to determine dimension or capacity. Also, an index number used to denote the thickness and weight of sheet metal.

GEL. — A jelly-like material formed by the coagulation of a colloidal liquid such as gum agar and gum tragacanth in preparation for enameling. The jellied solution should be thinned with water before using.

GLASS. — An amorphous, hard, brittle, often transparent material made by melting a mixture of the proper proportions of quartz, soda, and lime.

GLASS BEADS AND BALLS. — Used to fuse into an enamel surface for textural effects.

GLASS STRINGS. — Smelted transparent or opaque white, black or colored enamel strings used for texture.

GLOSS. — A term used to designate the shine or luster on a smooth enameled surface.

GLOVES. — Asbestos mittens and soft canvas finger variety. To protect hands from hot enamel objects.

GUM ARABIC. — A vegetable gum somewhat similar to tragacanth, though not as pure as the transparent high-grade tragacanth.

GUM TRAGACANTH. — A vegetable gum in flake form. It is dissolved and cooked with water and strained to a very thin watery solution. In this form it is applied to the metal surface with a camel's-hair brush as an adhesive for the powdered enamel.

HAMMER MARKS. — An even pattern of marks made on copper in shaping it. The final shaping, done with a rounded pean hammer, is called planishing.

HAMMERS. — Forming, raising, and planishing for metal work.

HARDNESS. — As applied to vitreous enamel; varies from soft melting enamels at 1000°F. to high-fired enamels melting at 1700°F. Copper enamels for art use are usually soft, medium, and hard; however, the range between all three is not very great.

HUE. — The predominating color of an enameled surface.

HYDRATION. — The act of moistening or impregnating with water. Application of water to dry surface of powdered enamel on an object.

HYDROFLUORIC ACID. — This acid attacks glass and is kept in wax bottles ;a solvent for silica.

INFUSIBLE. — That which cannot be fused or melted down.

INORGANIC. — This term is applied to all substances that do not contain carbon as a constituent; also to others in which carbon is present in an unimportant

153

sense, e.g., metallic carbonates. Metals, rocks, minerals and a variety of earths are all inorganic.

INSOLUBLE. — Incapable of dissolving in a liquid.

INSULATION. — Any material used to prevent the escape of heat, electricity or sound.

IRIDESCENT STAIN. — The term applied to a multicolored sheen which sometimes appears on lead-bearing enamels several months or years after the enamel has been fused. Most noticeable with dark blue, light turquoise, and emerald green.

IRON OXIDE. — Occurs in nature or may be manufactured. Used in production of ceramic colors, such as brown, black, and mahogany red.

KILN. — A large oven, usually of brick construction, which is heated for the purpose of hardening, burning, or drying pottery and other clay wares. (Not referred to in the enameled metal field.) Metal and enamel is fired in furnaces.

LACQUER. — Hard variety, applied with brush to highly polished metal parts or edges of bowls to protect the shine.

LAVENDER OIL. — An essential oil used in applying colors in painting enameling technique.

LEADBEARING. — A term specifically applied to enamel frits in which lead oxide is used as one of the principal fluxes.

LEADLESS. — Any material which does not contain lead is so described. Leadless enamels are used almost entirely in commercial opaque enamels.

LUMINOUS ENAMELS. — A term used to denote extreme depth and reflective quality of the metal surface shining up through the transparent enamel. Sulphides of calcium produce another form of luminous enamels.

LUSTER. — A pearly thin coating of metallic solution fused onto an opaque or transparent fired enamel surface. Silver, platinum, gold, copper and mother-of-pearl are common lusters.

MALLEABLE. — A metal which is capable of being hammered or shaped by hammering, or by pressure, is said to be malleable.

MANGANESE. — A grayish-pink lustrous, brittle metal, insoluble in water but decomposing in boiling water and soluble in acids. A constituent of cast iron and sheet metal.

MANGANESE DIOXIDE. — A raw material used in combination with other metals to produce blue and black colored enamels. Transparent lavender is produced with manganese dioxide .

MAT. — A slightly roughened surface almost or entirely lacking in luster.

MELTING POINT. — The temperature at which a solid changes to a liquid.

MESH. — The numerous small openings in a screen or sieve. A 200-mesh sieve has 200 openings per linear inch; an 80-mesh has 80 openings.

METAL BLISTER. — The bloating of a copper sheet in firing due to the presence of entrapped gas. Small quantities of zinc or lead in scrap-smelted copper will produce bad enameling blisters. Scrap copper is not suitable for art enameling.

MICA, OR ISINGLASS. — A native hydrous silicate which can be split into very thin transparent sheets. Used as backing for firing plique-à-jour art enamels. Will not burn in furnace temperature. Used to make enamel sheeting for eggshell.

MINERAL. — Any nonorganic or fossilized organic substance found in nature. Minerals have definite chemical compositions and are formed by the processes of inorganic reactions.

MOHS' SCALE OF HARDNESS. — The hardness of a mineral is gauged by its ability to scratch or be scratched by one of ten standard minerals: talc, gypsum, calcite, fluoride, apatite, orthoclase, quartz, topaz, corundum, diamond. Each mineral in the scale is scratched by the one following it.

MONEL METAL. — An acid-resisting nickel copper alloy used extensively in the enamel industry for pickling or firing equipment.

MORTAR. — Agate, porcelain or steel receptacle for use with pestle for grinding enamels.

MOTOR. — With spindles that hold polishing buffers.

MUSHROOM ANVIL OR IRON. — A hard steel iron in the shape of a mushroom; used in shaping metal bowls.

NICHROME. — A trade name. An alloy of nickel, iron, and chromium used in electric heating or resistance devices and acid resisting apparatus. It has a high melting point. Used for wiring electric enameling furnaces.

NITRIC ACID. — A strong acid. A colorless liquid, soluble in water. Prepared from Chile saltpeter, or by fixation of atmospheric nitrogen. Fuming nitric acid contains 86% nitric acid, concentrated contains 65% nitric acid. Concentrated nitric acid can cause severe burns quickly. Sometimes used in very dilute water solution for cleaning and pickling copper.

OILS. — China wood oil; a type sometimes used in making paste enamels. French fat oil; oil of turpentine used in painting enamels. Lavender oil; also used for painting enamels. Burns away, as do the others when the enamel reaches fusion temperature. Many different types of oils can be used for painters' enamel.

OPACIFYER. — Any material which gives or adds opacity to anything. Formerly tin oxide was the common opacifier for enamels; more recently antimony, zircon, and titanium compounds are used as opacifiers.

OPACITY. — Opaque enamels that fuse over and completely cover the base metal. An enamel is as opaque as its ability to reflect incident light.

OPALESCENT ENAMELS. — Enamels having a milky quality of iridescence when fired. Opaque enamels with transparent base often turn opalescent.

OPAQUE. — Anything which is not transparent but acts as an obscuring body.

OVEN. — Any heated chamber for drying enamels.

OVERBURNING. — A condition that sometimes occurs when enamel pieces are left more than three minutes in the furnace, or when the temperature is considerably above the regular firing point of 1500°F.

OXIDATION. — Discoloration of metal due to heat or oxygen.

OXIDE COLOR. — Mixtures of metallic pigments and certain fluxes are calcined and ground to a finely divided state. Chromium oxide, iron oxide, and cobalt oxide are some of the common metallic oxides used in the manufacture of color oxides.

PAILLONS. — Small pieces of die-stamped flowers, animals, birds, lines, stars, dots, circles, rosettes, etc., cut from silver and gold foil. Paillons can be fired into an enamel surface. Oftentimes transparent or clear enamels are fired over the top of the foil.

PAINTERS' ENAMEL. — Colored oxides finely ground with soft fusing clear enamel. (For painting on enamel surface with camel's-hair brush.)

PAPER. — Hard surfaced, glossy, thin, porous, transparent and waxed papers used for stencil cutting or for template making in simplified application of enamel colors to base enamel or metal surface.

154

PASTE. — Finely ground enamels mixed with pine oil or lavender oil for body. Turpentine added for painting with a brush.

PASTEL COLORS. — The term applied to pale or very weak colors.

PATINA. — The thin and often multicolored coat of oxides formed on metallic surfaces due to aging or peculiar atmospheric conditions.

PATTERNS. — Designs cut out of thin paper or thin lead sheeting for design and color application.

PESTLE. — A blunt and rounded instrument for pounding enamel frits in a mortar.

PICKLING. — The practice of treating copper, silver, aluminum and other metals with acid and water solution to prepare them for successful enameling.

PIGMENTS. — Insoluble colored substances used as bases in compounding ceramic or enamel colors.

PINE OIL. — Tacky medium used for painting enamels.

PLANCH. — A coarse wire mesh to hold an enamel piece being fired. Finer mesh screen is called a sieve.

PLANISHING. — A surface treatment by hammering in finishing a metal bowl or surface of metal sheeting.

PLATING. — Any process by which a surface is coated with a metal, as silver plating, nickel plating, gold plating. It is possible to enamel silver-plated copper or steel with low-temperature enamels successfully.

PLATINUM. — A silver gray metal, insoluble in water, nitric or hydrochloric acid, but soluble in aqua regia. Can be purchased in leaf and liquid form and used for decorating fired enameled surfaces. To fuse at 1350°F.

PLIQUE-À-JOUR ENAMELING. — A type of artistic enameling in which the piece when finished appears as stained-glass window.

PROPANE. — A colorless gas used in hand torches as a quick means for fusing small enamels, jewelry, etc.

PUMICE. — Pumice stone. A light porous stone of volcanic origin which consists of silicates of aluminum, sodium, and potassium. It is used as an abrasive in powder or stone form to grind down the high surface of cloisonné enamels. Also used for cleaning and polishing metal.

PYROMETER. — An instrument for measuring degrees of heat above those indicated by the mercurial thermometers. Successful enameling needs the use of a pyrometer for measuring exact temperature.

RESIST. — Any material, usually asphaltum, used in the etching process to cover and protect areas that are not to be acid etched.

RESPIRATOR. A face mask which is worn to prevent ceramic and enamel workers from inhaling injurious pickle fumes or enamel dust.

RHEOSTAT. — An instrument for regulating the supply of electric current.

ROUGE. — Red compound for putting high polish on metals with cloth buffer and motor.

RUBBING STONES. — A fine, hard abrasive material in the form of square or long blocks used to remove imperfections in enamel surface and to remove fired enamel and scale from edge of bowls, plaques, and jewelry.

SANDBLASTING. — The operation of cleaning sheet copper, cast iron or steel by spraying silica sand onto the metal with compressed air.

SCALE. — A defect caused when metallic oxide imbeds itself in the enamel surface either before, during or after firing. Such scale usually comes from burning tools, trivets, etc. Such defects can usually be covered up by a final coat of opaque enamel. Such

troubles in transparent surfaces completely ruin the work.

SCRIBER. — A sharp-pointed steel instrument used for engraving metal surfaces.

SCUM. — The impurities that rise to the surface of molten materials.

SEMIMAT FINISH. — An enameled surface not altogether rough to the touch but having a slight, glossy appearance.

SEMITRANSPARENT. — An enamel which is partly opaque and not totally transparent, as on opalescent enamel surfaces.

SGRAFFITO. — A technique in enameling earlier used in pottery and ceramic wares, where a linear drawing is scratched through the top enamel surface to reach a contrasting fired surface underneath.

SHADING. — A pleasant gradation effect in enamel by sifting a light application of dark enamel powder over a lighter color, or vice versa. This can be applied with gum solution, powdered enamel, and a sieve.

SHEARS. — Tinning shears for cutting metals.

SIEVE. — Any screen that is used to separate particles according to size. Usually made of steel, brass or copper.

SILT. — The gray and cloudy material that rises to the surface when washing powdered enamels.

SLIP ENAMEL. — The ground liquid enamel as it comes from the mill after the wet grinding operation. Sometimes called slush.

SMELTING. — The process of melting enamel raw materials in a smelting furnace around 2500°F. The raw materials which have been first thoroughly mixed, are loaded into a smelter and allowed to stay there until thoroughly and uniformly melted. Stirring the batch with a clean nickel rod is done often. The melting process usually requires from one to three hours at the above temperature.

SODIUM FLUORIDE. — Used to a small extent as a fluxing enamel raw material; also used to produce a milky opacity in the enamel.

SOLDER. — A fusing metal or alloy that is used to unite adjacent surfaces of less fusible metals or alloys. Hard silver solder is used for enameling as it can withstand furnace heat without coming apart. Soft solders can be used for brooch needle backs, cuff links, etc.

SPATULA. — A blunt flexible knife used for mixing semi-solid masses working up painters' enamel for correct consistency and workability on a glass slab.

SPINNING. — An operation whereby sheet metal is rotated on a lathe forcing it to flow by means of a round tool pressed against it. Wood forms used are called chucks.

SPOT WELDING. — Two pieces of metal are united by heating to the molten state and fixing them together permanently.

SQUEEGEE OIL. — A special mixture of oils used to suspend enamel color in paste form. This oil will burn off during the firing process. Used in painters' technique.

STAKE. — Mushroom or T stake in assorted sizes for forming or hammering sheet copper, for planishing metal surfaces.

STAMPING. — A method of shaping metal sheets into shapes for enameling. All metals can be die-stamped.

STEEL WOOL. — For polishing copper surfaces.

STENCIL. — Sometimes called a "template." A pattern which may be cut from paper, cardboard, sheet zinc, or other thin metals and used for applying enamel designs to metal.

STENCIL BRUSH. — A flat, hard, bristle brush used to pound black, white or colored paste enamels onto an already fired surface.

STENCIL KNIFE. — A sharp-pointed knife used for cutting stencils. Surgical knives and single-edge razors are also often used.

STILTS. — Small point bars in assorted shapes and designs made from pottery clay bodies, used to support the piece being fired in the furnace. Some stilts come with sharp wire points.

STONES. — Corundum or alundum, for stoning enamel surface and metal edges.

SULPHURIC ACID. — A strong acid made by uniting sulphur dioxide and oxygen; then combining the resultant trioxide with water to form the finished acid. A solution of 6% sulphuric acid in a warm state is used for pickling copper prior to enameling. Remember always to pour the acid into the water, *not* the water into the acid.

TAR. — A thick brown to black liquid with distinctive odor, obtained from the distillation of wood, peat, coal, shale and other vegetable or mineral materials. It consists of a mixture of hydrocarbons and their derivatives. Sometimes used to black out portions of metal not to be etched with acid.

TEARING. — An enamel coat applied and fused that tears away from undercoat, usually because of firing while too damp, or an enamel coat applied too heavily.

TEMPLATE. — An outline of a pattern to be cut out of paper, wax paper, cardboard or thin metal.

THERMOSTAT. — An automatic instrument for indicating or regulating temperatures. A device so affected by heat that it makes or breaks electrical contacts by mechanical means.

TIMER. — A special alarm clock which can be set to ring at fractions of a minute. Necessary for the adequate firing of art objects. A valuable asset to good work.

TONGS. — A laboratory appliance for holding hot objects such as screens holding art objects entering furnace, crucibles, etc.

TORCH. — Master torch, propane, 'Burnz-O-Matic' torch for quick fusing of small enamels.

TRAGACANTH. — A gum flake, organic in nature, cooked with water and thinned through cheesecloth or a fine mesh sieve. It is applied to metal surfaces in the application of enamel powder by the sifting process. Acts as an adhesive. (Use pure flake for best results. Purchased in all drug stores.)

TRIPOD. — A three-legged support for holding nickel firing screen and enamel object over burner or for easy fusing of enamel on small articles of jewelry with a propane torch.

TRIVET. — Metal supports made of chromel steel to hold enamel while firing. (Scale proof.)

TURNTABLE. — A circular platform designed to turn upon its center axis and used to hold plates and bowls for the easy tooling of lines or banding of colors or liquid golds and lusters. Operated manually by small slow moving belt connected to a motor.

TURQUOISE. — A hydrous phosphate of aluminum, colored blue by a copper compound. A color given to greenish-blue enamel.

TWEEZERS. — Long variety used to pick up small bits of solder and texture particles.

URANIUM OXIDE. — Is amphoteric and forms the "uranates" with bases and the "uranyl" salts with acids. Used to produce vibrant yellow-orange enamel.

VALUE. — In color comparison, the quality by which a light color is distinguished from a dark color.

VARIABLE. — A factor that is not constant but changing.

VICE. — Heavy-duty bench size or small table size for holding work in process.

VISCOUS. — Sticky or gummy.

VITREOUS ENAMEL. — A glassy composition applied to metal and fused at a low red to bright red heat at approximately 1500°F. Although it is glass, it adheres to metal and resists punishment both by impact and by rapid changes of temperature. This requirement necessitates the addition of other ingredients besides those used in the manufacture of ordinary glass such as window glass, bottle glass or plate glass. Opaque enamels are less fragile than transparent enamels. Enamel on soft copper is more susceptible to damage than enamel on heavier copper or steel.

VITRIFICATION. — The changing into glass or glassy substance by heat and fusion.

VOLATILE. — A substance that evaporates rapidly is said to be volatile.

WARPING. — The change in the original contour of a piece of enameled metal due to the firing operation, handling while placing piece from the hot trivet, or burning pins to a suitably hard, fireproof, flat surface. Hot pieces can be handled with asbestos mittens. Warping can be rectified between the time the piece leaves the trivet and when it is flat on a table surface of hard rock asbestos. This must be done quickly before the piece beings to cool and lose its flexibility.

WEATHERING. — Chemical and physical reactions of air, water, bacteria, heat and freezing which will disintegrate material and change its composition. Opaque, acid-resisting enamels weather better over a period of time than the usual high-lead transparent copper enamels.

WET GRINDING. — Enamel, water, and clay combination ground in a ball mill to produce slip or slush enamel.

ZIRCON SAND. — "Zirconium silicate," the natural zircon-bearing material found in Australia, India, and Florida.